RICHARD OF JAMESTOWN

A Story of Virginia Colony

RICHARD OF JAMESTOWN
A story of Virginia Colony

BY

JAMES OTIS

with illustrations by
C.W. Kamis

LIVING BOOKS PRESS
MOUNT PLEASANT, MICHIGAN

This edition is an unabridged re-publication of the work by James Otis Kaler, with many pen and ink illustrations by C.W. Kamis, originally published by American Book Company in 1910.

LIVING BOOKS PRESS
Publishers of classic *living* books.
5497 S. Gilmore Road
Mt. Pleasant, Michigan 48858
www.livingbookscurriculum.com

Cover and arrangement © 2007 Living Books Press

ISBN-13: 978-0-9790876-0-8

Printed in the United States of America

A NOTE TO THE HOME EDUCATOR

THE *COLONIAL AMERICA SERIES*

Living Books Curriculum is pleased to make available this series of books on Colonial America by James Otis (1848-1912). Otis was a writer, educator and historian who wrote over 150 books for children. He wrote the *Colonial America Series* to illustrate for children the home life of colonists. Otis felt history books did not adequately describe the fascinating details of this time in American history:

"Surely it is entertaining as well as instructive for young people to read of the toil and privations in the homes of those who came into a new world to build up a country for themselves, and such homely facts are not to be found in the real histories of our land."

We believe that children should experience history through literature because the people and events in a well-written story are real in the child's imagination. The future of the characters becomes significant to him; thus, history itself becomes meaningful and memorable.

Young children live their history on a day-to-day basis. They have a narrow perspective on historical events, even as far back as their own birth. This is why a child asks you to tell and retell the stories from his own life. He can then live the story in his own mind and play it in his games. To a child, "story" is history.

NARRATION

NARRATION IS A SIMPLE YET POWERFUL TOOL of learning that can be used throughout the reading of the *Colonial America Series,* as well as any quality literature. Most children enjoy telling what they know about a subject. It delights them to relate an incident, however small it may seem to us. Educational reformer Charlotte Mason believed that this love of telling could be used as a foundation for self-education.

Narration is retelling in one's own words what has just been read (either aloud or silently). It is a natural way for a child to demonstrate learning and to organize information. Narration requires an independence that expects the child to work through the material on his own rather than depending on the person teaching to pick out the important points through appropriate questions. Narration may be done in many forms, but the most beneficial to the student is oral retelling. Because of the increased need for oral communication in our society, learning to be verbal at an early age is a valuable skill. Narration is one method that provides an outstanding opportunity for your child to develop expressive skills.

When you are ready to do narration, sit with your child (this also works with more than one child) and say gently with a smile, "I am going to read (give the title) one time to you. I want you to listen carefully. Then tell me in your own words all you remember of the story." After you have read the story, pause a moment and let it settle in, then say, "Tell me all you remember about the story." At this point, listen without comment until the child is done. If there is more than one child, you can let one start and the others continue. Or, alternately, you can have the first child narrate and then ask the second (or third), "Is there anything you would like to add?" Taking turns narrating while others listen builds the habit of attention in children.

The *Colonial America Series* is ideal for narration because Otis uses short chapters. Children ages eight and up can narrate one of these chapters with a bit of practice. However, a child of six or seven should narrate single paragraphs until he is able to retell with ease, then the passage length can be increased.

Narration, if done consistently and correctly, gives your child beauty of expression, recall of material, increased mental facility, and a means of evaluating what is understood.

If you would like to read a complete article describing the process, visit the Living Books Curriculum website: <www.livingbookscurriculum.com/successfulnarration.htm>

CORRELATION OF LESSONS

To CORRELATE MEANS to bring one thing into a complementary relation with another. To correlate studies means to bring one subject, such as history or science, into a complementary relationship with another, such as art or nature study. Charlotte Mason felt correlated studies enable greater exploration of ideas and ought not to result in "busy work". (*A Philosophy of Education*, p. 114, ff)

Copywork, spelling, science, homemaking, handwork, math, dictation, geography are all areas of the curriculum that are enhanced by using the *Colonial America Series* as a starting point. Each book in the series references everyday skills, foods, customs, expressions and place names. For copywork, choose a particularly language-rich passage, and have your child practice penmanship by transcribing it. For geography, have your child discover on a map of the United States each of the place names. For spelling, note unfamiliar words during the reading and make these the subject of a spelling quiz once a week. For vocabulary building, take the same words used for spelling and have your child enter them and their definitions in a notebook.

MORE IN THE COLONIAL AMERICA SERIES

IF YOU ENJOY THIS BOOK and would like to read others in the series, or other high-quality literature, visit the Living Books Curriculum website: <www.livingbookscurriculum.com>.

Children have a right to the best we possess; therefore their lesson books should be, as far as possible, our best books.
Charlotte Mason, *A Philosophy of Education*

Sheila Carroll
Mount Pleasant, Michigan

FOREWARD

THE PURPOSE OF THIS SERIES OF STORIES is to show the children, and even those who have already taken up the study of history, the *home life* of the colonists with whom they meet in their books. To this end every effort has been made to avoid anything savoring of romance, and to deal only with facts, so far as it is possible, while describing the daily life of those people who conquered the wilderness whether for conscience sake or for gain.

That the stories may appeal more directly to the children, they are told from the viewpoint of a child, and purport to have been related by a child. Should any criticism be made regarding the seeming neglect to mention important historical facts, the answer would be that these books are not sent out as histories,—although it is believed that they will awaken a desire to learn more of the building of the nation,— and only such incidents as would be particularly noted by a child are used.

Surely it is entertaining as well as instructive for young people to read of the toil and privations in the homes of those who came into a new world to build up a country for themselves, and such homely facts are not to be found in the real histories of our land.

James Otis.

CONTENTS

Who I am 1
Left Alone in the World 2
An Idle Boy 3
Captain John Smith Comes to London 3
Meeting Captain Smith 5
Captain Smith Speaks to Me 6
The Plans of the London Company 8
The Vessels of the Fleet 9
How I Earned my Passage 10
When the Fleet Set Sail 11
The Voyage Delayed 12
Nathaniel's Story 14
We Make Sail Again 16
The First Island 17
Captain Smith Accused 18
Captain Smith a Prisoner 18
I Attend my Master 19
Several Islands Visited 20
A Variety of Wild Game 22
The Tempest 24
The New Country Sighted 24
The Leader not Known 25
Arrival at Chesapeake Bay 26
An Attack by the Savages 28
Reading the London Company's Orders 29
Captain Smith a Member of the Council 31

Captain Smith Forced to Remain Aboard 32
Exploring the Country 33
The People Land from the Ships 36
Captain Smith Proven Innocent 37
We who were Left Behind 38
Baking Bread without Ovens 39
An Unequal Division of Labor 40
Building a House of Logs 41
Keeping House 43
Lack of Cleanliness in the Village 44
Cave Homes 45
The Golden Fever 46
Ducks and Oysters 47
Roasting Oysters 48
Learning to Cook Other Things 49
The Sweet Potato Root 51
A Touch of Homesickness 52
Master Hunt's Preaching 53
Neglecting to Provide for the Future 54
Surprised by Savages 55
Strengthening the Fort 56
A Time of Sickness and Death 57
Captain Smith Gains Authority 58
Disagreeable Measures of Discipline 60
Signs of Rebellion 62
The Second Proclamation 63
Building a Fortified Village 64
Trapping Turkeys 65
A Crude Kind of Chimney 67

Cooking a Turkey	68
Candles or Rushlights	70
The Visit of Pocahontas	71
Captain Kendall's Plot	73
The Death of Captain Kendall	74
Captain Smith's Expedition and Return	75
An Exciting Adventure	76
Taken before Powhatan	78
Pocahontas Begs for Smith's Life	79
The Effect of Captain Smith's Return	80
A New Church	82
Captain Newport's Return	83
Gold-Seekers	85
A Worthless Cargo	86
The Condition of the Colony	87
Tobacco	88
Captain Newport's Return	90
Gazing at the Women	91
Master Hunt Brings Great news	92
Captain Newport's Instructions	93
The Story of Roanoke	94
The Crowning of Powhatan	96
Preparing for the Future	97
Stealing the Company's Goods	99
What the Thieving Led to	100
Fear of Famine in a Land of Plenty	101
The Unhealthful Location	102
Gathering Oysters	103
Preparing Sturgeon for Food	104

Turpentine and Tar	104
The Making of Clapboards	106
Providing for the Children	107
Dreams of the Future	108
A Plague of Rats	109
Treachery During Captain Smith's Absence	110
Captain Smith's Speech	111
The New Laws	112
The Accident	113
Captain Smith's Departure	114
The "Starving Time"	116
Our Courage Gives Out	117
Abandoning Jamestown	118
Lord de la Warr's Arrival	119
The Young Planters	120

RICHARD OF JAMESTOWN

WHO I AM

YES, MY NAME IS RICHARD MUTTON. Sounds rather queer, doesn't it? The lads in London town used to vex me sorely by calling, "Baa, baa, black sheep," whenever I passed them, and yet he who will may find the name Richard Mutton written in the list of those who were sent to Virginia, in the new world, by the London Company, on the nineteenth day of December, in the year of Our Lord, 1606.

Whosoever may chance to read what I am here setting down, will, perhaps, ask how it happened that a lad only ten years of age was allowed to sail for that new world in company with such a band of adventurous men as headed the enterprise.

Therefore it is that I must tell a certain portion of the story of my life, for the better understanding of how I came to be in this fair, wild, savage beset land of Virginia.

Yet I was not the only boy who sailed in the *Susan Constant*, as you may see by turning to the list of names, which is under the care, even to this day, of the London Company, for there you will find written in clerkly hand the names Samuel Collier, Nathaniel Peacock, James Brumfield, and Richard Mutton.

Nathaniel Peacock has declared more than once that my name comes last in the company at the very end of all, because I was not a full grown mutton; but only large enough to be called a sheep's tail, and therefore should be hung on behind, as is shown by the list.

LEFT ALONE IN THE WORLD

The reason of my being in this country of Virginia at so young an age, is directly concerned with that brave soldier and wondrous adventurer, Captain John Smith, of whom I make no doubt the people in this new world, when the land has been covered with towns and villages, will come to know right well, for of a truth he is a wonderful man.

In the sixth month of Grace, 1606, I was living as best I might in that great city of London, which is as much a wilderness of houses, as this country is a wilderness of trees.

My father was a soldier of fortune, which means that he stood ready to do battle in behalf of whatsoever nation he believed was in the right, or, perhaps, on the side of those people who would pay him the most money for risking his life.

He had fought with the Dutch soldiers under command of one Captain Miles Standish, an Englishman of renown among men of arms, and had been killed.

My mother died less than a week before the news was brought that my father had been shot to death. Not then fully understanding how great a disaster it is to a young lad when he loses father or mother, and how yet more sad is his lot when he has lost both parents, I made shift to live as best I might with a sore heart; but yet not so sore as if I had known the full extent of the misfortune which had overtaken me.

AN IDLE BOY

AT FIRST IT WAS AN EASY MATTER FOR ME to get food at the home of this lad, or of that, among my acquaintances, sleeping wherever night overtook me; but, finally, when mayhap three months had gone by, my welcome was worn threadbare, and I was told by more than one, that a hulking lad of ten years should have more pride than to beg his way from door to door.

It is with shame I here set down the fact, that many weeks passed before I came to understand, in ever so slight a degree, what a milksop I must be, thus eating the bread of idleness when I should have won the right, by labor, to a livelihood in this world.

This last thought had just begun to take root in my heart when Nathaniel Peacock, whose mother had been a good friend of mine during a certain time after I was made an orphan, and I, heard that a remarkably brave soldier was in the city of London, making ready to go into the new world, with the intent to build there a town for the king.

CAPTAIN JOHN SMITH COMES TO LONDON

THIS MAN WAS NO OTHER than Captain John Smith, who, although at this time not above six and twenty years of age, had already served in the French, in the Dutch, and in the Transylvanian armies, where he had met and overcome many dangers.

He had been robbed and beaten

and thrown into the sea because of not believing in the religion of the men who attacked him; he had been a slave among the Turks; he had fought, one after another, three of the bravest in the Turkish army, and had cut off the head of each in turn.

Can it be wondered at that Nathaniel Peacock and I were filled to overflowing with admiration for this wonderful soldier, or that we desired above all things to see him?

We loitered about the streets of London town from daylight until night had come again, hoping to feast our eyes upon this same John Smith, who was to us one of the wonders of the world, because in so short a time he had made his name as a soldier famous in all countries, and yet we saw him not.

We had searched London town over and over for mayhap a full month, doing nothing else save hunt for the man whose life had been so filled with adventure, and each time we returned home, Mistress Peacock reproached me with being an idle good-for-nothing, and Nathaniel but little better.

I believe it was her harsh words which caused to spring up in my heart a desire to venture into the new world, where it was said gold could be found in abundance, and even the smallest lad might pick up whatsoever of wealth he desired, if so be his heart was strong enough to brave the journey across the great ocean.

The more I thought of what could be found in that land, which was called Virginia, the stronger grew my desire, until the time came when it was a fixed purpose in my mind, and not until then did I breathe to Nathaniel a word of that which had been growing within me.

He took fire straightway I spoke of what it might be possible for us lads to do, and declared that whether his mother were willing or no, he would brave all the dangers of that terrible journey over-seas, if so be we found an opportunity.

To him it seemed a simple matter that, having once found a ship which was to sail for the far-off land, we might hide ourselves within her, having gathered sufficient of food to keep us alive during the journey. But how this last might be done, his plans had not been made.

MEETING CAPTAIN SMITH

Lest I should set down too many words, and therefore bring upon myself the charge of being one who can work with his tongue better than with his hands, I will pass over all that which Nathaniel and I did during the long time we roamed the streets, in the hope of coming face to face with Captain Smith.

It is enough if I set it down at once that we finally succeeded in our purpose, having come upon him one certain morning on Cheapside, when there was a fight on among some apprentices, and the way so blocked that neither he nor any other could pass through the street, until the quarrelsome fellows were done playing upon each other's heads with sticks and stones.

It seemed much as if fortune had at last consented to smile upon us, for we were standing directly in front of the great man.

I know not how it chanced that I, a lad whose apparel was far from being either cleanly or whole, should have dared to raise my voice in speech with one who was said to have talked even with a king. Yet so I did, coming without many words to that matter which had been growing these many days in my mind, and mayhap it was the very suddenness of the words that caught his fancy.

"Nathaniel Peacock and I are minded to go with you into that new world, Captain John Smith, if so be you permit us," I said, "and there we will serve you with honesty and industry."

CAPTAIN SMITH SPEAKS TO ME

THERE WAS A SMILE COME UPON HIS FACE as I spoke, and he looked down upon Nathaniel and me, who were wedged among that throng which watched the apprentices quarrel, until we were like to be squeezed flat, and said in what I took to be a friendly tone:

"So, my master, you would journey into Virginia with the hope of making yourself rich, and you not out from under your mother's apron as yet?"

"I have no mother to wear an apron, Captain Smith, nor father to say I may go there or shall come here; but yet would serve you as keenly as might any man, save mayhap my strength, which will increase, be not so great as would be found in those older."

Whether this valiant soldier was pleased with my words, or if in good truth boys were needed in the enterprise, I cannot say; but certain it is he spoke to me fairly, writing down upon a piece of paper, which he tore from his tablets, the name of the street in which he had lodgings, and asking, as he handed it to me, if I could read.

Now it was that I gave silent thanks, because of what had seemed to me a hardship when my mother forced me to spend so many hours each day in learning to use a quill, until I was able to write a clerkly hand.

It seemed to please this great soldier that I could do what few of the lads in that day had been taught to master, and, without further ado, he said to me boldly:

"You shall journey into Virginia with me, an' it please you, lad. What is more, I will take upon myself the charge of outfitting you, and time shall tell whether you have enough of manliness in you to repay me the cost."

Then it was that Nathaniel raised his voice; but the captain gave him no satisfaction, declaring it was the duty of a true lad to stand by his mother, and that he would lend his aid to none who had a home, and in it those who cared for him.

I could have talked with this brave soldier until the night had come, and would never have wearied of asking concerning what might be found in that new world of Virginia; but it so chanced that when the business was thus far advanced, the apprentices were done with striving to break each other's heads, and Captain Smith, bidding me come to his house next morning, went his way.

THE PLANS OF THE LONDON COMPANY

THEN IT WAS THAT NATHANIEL DECLARED he also would go on the voyage to Virginia, whether it pleased Captain Smith or no, and I, who should have set my face against his running away from home, spoke no word to oppose him, because it would please me to have him as comrade.

After this I went more than once to the house where Captain Smith lodged, and learned very much concerning what it was proposed to do toward building a town in the new world.

Both Nathaniel and I had believed it was the king who counted to send all these people over-seas; but I learned from my new master that a company of London merchants was in charge of the enterprise, these merchants believing much profit might come to them in the way of getting gold.

The whole business was to be under the control of Captain Bartholomew Gosnold, who, it was said, had already made one voyage to the new world, and had brought back word that it was a goodly place in which to settle and to build up towns. The one chosen to act as admiral of the fleet, for there were to be three ships instead of one, as I had fancied, was Captain Christopher Newport, a man who had no little fame as a seaman.

In due time, as the preparations for the voyage were being

forwarded, I was sent by my master into lodgings at Blackwall, just below London town, for the fleet lay nearby, and because it was understood by those in charge of the adventure that I was in Captain Smith's service, no hindrance was made to my going on board the vessels.

THE VESSELS OF THE FLEET

THESE WERE THREE IN NUMBER, as I have already said: the *Susan Constant,* a ship of near to one hundred tons in size; the *Goodspeed*, of forty tons, and the *Discovery*, which was a pinnace of only twenty tons.

And now, lest some who read what I have set down may not be acquainted with the words used by seamen, let me explain that the

The "Susan Constant"

measurement of a vessel by tons, means that she will fill so much space in the water. Now, in measuring a vessel, a ton is reckoned as forty cubic feet of space, therefore when I say the *Susan Constant* was one hundred tons in size, it is the same as if I had set down that she would carry four thousand cubic feet of cargo.

That he who reads may know what I mean by a pinnace, as differing from a ship, I can best make it plain by saying that such a craft is an open boat, wherein may be used sails or oars, and, as in the case of the *Discovery*, may have a deck over a certain portion of her length. That our pinnace was a vessel able to withstand such waves as would be met with in the ocean, can be believed when you remember that she was one half the size of the *Goodspeed,* which we counted a ship.

The "Goodspeed"

The "Discovery"

HOW I EARNED MY PASSAGE

Captain Smith, my master, found plenty of work for me during the weeks before the fleet sailed. He had many matters to be set down in writing, and because of my mother's care in teaching me to use the quill, I was able, or so it seemed to me, to be of no little aid to him in those busy days, when it was as if he must do two or three things at the same time in order to bring his business to an end.

I learned during that time to care very dearly for this valiant soldier, who could, when the fit was on him, be as tender and kind as a girl, and again, when he was crossed, as stern a man as one might find in all London town.

Because of my labors, and it pleased me greatly that I could do somewhat toward forwarding the adventure, I had no time in which to search for my friend, Nathaniel Peacock, although I did not cease to hope that he would try to find me.

I had parted with him in the city, and he knew right well where I was going; yet, so far as I could learn, he had never come to Blackwall.

I had no doubt but that I could find him in the city, and it was in my mind, at the first opportunity, to seek him out, if for no other reason than that we might part as comrades should, for he had been a true friend to me when my heart was sore; but from the moment the sailors began to put the cargo on board the *Susan Constant* and the *Goodspeed*, I had no chance to wander around Blackwall, let alone journeying to London town.

WHEN THE FLEET SET SAIL

Then came the twentieth of December, when we were to set sail, and great was the rejoicing among the people, who believed that we would soon build up a city in the new world, which would be of great wealth and advantage to those in England.

I heard it said, although I myself was not on shore to see what was done, that in all the churches prayers were made for our safe journeying, and there was much marching to and fro of soldiers, as if some great merrymaking were afoot.

The shore was lined with people; booths were set up where showmen displayed for pay many curious things, and food and sweetmeats were on sale here and there, for so large a throng stood in need of refreshment as well as amusement.

It was a wondrous spectacle to see all these people nearby on the shore, knowing they had come for no other purpose than to look at us, and I took no little pride to myself because of being numbered among the adventurers, even vainly fancying that many wondered what part a boy could have in such an undertaking.

Then we set sail, I watching in vain for a glimpse of Nathaniel Peacock as the ships got under way. Finally, sadly disappointed, and with the sickness of home already in my heart, I went into the forward part of the ship, where was my sleeping place, thinking that very shortly we should be tossing and tumbling on the mighty waves of the ocean.

THE VOYAGE DELAYED

IN THIS I WAS MISTAKEN, for the wind was contrary to our purpose, and we lay in the Downs near six weeks, while Master Hunt, the preacher, who had joined the company that he might labor for the good of our souls; lay so nigh unto death in the cabin of the *Susan Constant*, that I listened during all the waking hours of the night, fearing to hear the tolling of the ship's bell, which would tell that he had gone from among the living.

It was on the second night, after we were come to anchor in the

Downs awaiting a favorable wind, that I having fallen asleep while wishing Nathaniel Peacock might have been with us, was awakened by the pressure of a cold hand upon my cheek.

I was near to crying aloud with fear, for the first thought that came was that Master Hunt had gone from this world, and was summoning me; but before the cry could escape my lips, I heard the whispered words:

"It is me, Nate Peacock!"

It can well be guessed that I was sitting bolt upright in the narrow bed, which sailors call a bunk, by the time this had been said, and in the gloom of the seamen's living place I saw a head close to mine.

Not until I had passed my hands over the face could I believe it was indeed my comrade, and it goes without saying that straightway I insisted on knowing how he came there, when he should have been in London town.

I cannot set the story down as Nathaniel Peacock told it to me on that night, because his words were many; but the tale ran much like this:

NATHANIEL'S STORY

When Captain John Smith had promised on Cheapside that I should be one of the company of adventurers, because of such labor as it might be possible for me to perform, and had refused to listen to my comrade, Nathaniel, without acquainting me with the fact, had made up his mind that he also would go into the new world of Virginia.

Fearing lest I would believe it my duty to tell Captain Smith of his purpose, he kept far from me, doing whatsoever he might in London town to earn as much as would provide him with food during a certain time.

In this he succeeded so far as then seemed necessary, and when it was known that the fleet was nearly ready to make sail, he came to Blackwall with all his belongings tied in his doublet.

To get on board the *Susan Constant* without attracting much attention while she was being visited by so many curious people, was not a hard task for Nathaniel Peacock, and three days before the fleet was got under way, my comrade had hidden himself in the very foremost part of the ship, where were stored the ropes and chains.

There he had remained until thirst, or hunger, drove him out, on this night of which I am telling you, and he begged that I go on deck, where were the scuttle butts, to get him a pannikin of water.

For those of you who may not know what a scuttle butt is, I will explain that it is a large cask in which fresh water is kept on shipboard. When Nathaniel's burning thirst had been soothed, he began to fear that I might give information to Captain John Smith concerning him; but after all that had been done in the way of hiding himself, and remembering his suffering, I had not the heart so to do.

During four days more he spent all the hours of sunshine, and the greater portion of the night, in my bed, closely covered so that the sailors might not see him, and then came the discovery, when he was dragged out with many a blow and harsh word to give an account of himself. I fear it would have gone harder still with Nathaniel, if I had not happened to be there at that very moment.

As it was, I went directly to Captain John Smith, my master, telling him all Nathaniel's story, and asking if the lad had not shown himself made of the proper stuff to be counted on as one of the adventurers.

Although hoping to succeed in my pleading, I was surprised when the captain gave a quick consent to number the lad among those who were to go into the new land of Virginia, and was even astonished when his name was written down among others as if he had been pledged to the voyage in due form.

But for the sickness of Master Hunt, and the fear we had lest he should die, Nathaniel and I might have made exceeding merry while we lay at anchor in the Downs, for food was plentiful; there was little of work to be done, and we lads could have passed the time skylarking with such of the sailors as were disposed to sport, except orders had been given that no undue noise be made on deck.

WE MAKE SAIL AGAIN

It seemed to me almost as if we spent an entire lifetime within sight of the country we were minded to leave behind us, and indeed six weeks, with no change of scene, and while one is held to the narrow limits of a ship, is an exceeding long time.

However, as I have heard Captain Smith say again and again, everything comes to him who waits, and so also came that day when the winds were favoring; when Captain Newport, the admiral of our fleet, gave the word to make sail, and we sped softly away from England's shores, little dreaming of that time of suffering, of sickness, and of sadness which was before us.

To Nathaniel and me, who had never strayed far from London town, and knew no more of the sea than might have been gained in a boatman's wherry, the ocean was exceeding unkind, and for eight and forty hours did we lie in that narrow bed, believing death was very near at hand.

There is no reason why I should make any attempt at describing the sickness which was upon us, for I have since heard that it comes to all who go out on the sea for the first time. When we recovered, it was suddenly, like as a flower lifts up its head after a refreshing shower that has pelted it to the ground.

I would I might set down here all which came to us during the voyage, for it was filled with wondrous happenings; but because I would tell of what we did in the land of Virginia, I must be sparing of words now.

THE FIRST ISLAND

It is to be remembered that our fleet left London on the twentieth day of December, and, as I have since heard Captain Smith read from the pages which he wrote concerning the voyage, it was on the twenty-third of March that we were come to the island of Martinique, where for the first time Nathaniel Peacock and I saw living savages.

When we were come to anchor, they paddled out to our ships in frail boats called canoes, bringing many kinds of most delicious fruits, which we bought for such trumpery things as glass beads and ornaments of copper.

It was while we lay off this island that we saw a whale attacked and killed by a thresher and a swordfish, which was a wondrous sight.

CAPTAIN SMITH ACCUSED

AND NOW WAS A MOST WICKED DEED DONE by those who claimed to be in command of our company, for they declared that my master had laid a plot with some of the men in each vessel of the fleet, whereby the principal members of the company were to be murdered, to the end that Captain Smith might set himself up as king after we were come to the new world.

All this was untrue, as I knew full well, having aided him in such work as a real clerk would have done, and had there been a plot, I must have found some inkling of it in one of the many papers I read aloud to him, or copied down on other sheets that the work of the quill might be more pleasing to the eye.

Besides that, I had been with the captain a goodly portion of the time while the ships were being made ready for the voyage, and if he had harbored so much of wickedness, surely must some word of it have come to me, who sat or stood near at hand, listening attentivewhenever he had speech with others of the company of adventurers.

CAPTAIN SMITH A PRISONER

WHEN THE VOYAGE WAS BEGUN, and the captain no longer had need of me, I was sent into the forward part of the ship to live, as has already been set down, and therefore it was I knew nothing of what was being done in the great cabin, where the leaders of the company were quartered, until after my master was made a prisoner.

Then it was told me by the seaman who had been called by Captain Kendall, as if it was feared my master, being such a great soldier, might strive to harm those who miscalled him a traitor to that which he had sworn.

It seems, so the seaman said, that Captain John Martin was the one who made the charges against my master, on the night after we set sail from Martinique, when all the chief men of the company were met in the great cabin, and he declared that, when it was possible to do so, meaning after we had come to the land of Virginia, witnesses should be brought from the other ships to prove the wicked intent.

Then it was that Captain George Kendall declared my master must be kept a close prisoner until the matter could be disposed of, and all the others, save Captain Bartholomew Gosnold, agreeing, heavy irons were put upon him. He was shut up in his sleeping place, having made no outcry nor attempt to do any harm, save that he declared himself innocent of wrong doing.

But for Captain Gosnold and Master Hunt, the preacher, I should not have been permitted to go in and learn if I might do anything for his comfort. The other leaders declared that my master was a dangerous man, who should not be allowed to have speech with any person save themselves, lest he send some message to those who were said to be concerned with him in the plot.

I ATTEND MY MASTER

MASTER HUNT SPOKE UP RIGHT MANFULLY in behalf of Captain Smith, with the result that I was given free entrance to that small room which had been made his prison, save that I must at all times leave the door open, so those who were in the great cabin could hear if I was charged with any message to the seamen.

My eyes were filled with tears when my master told me that he had no thought save that of benefiting those who were with him in the adventure, and that he would not lend his countenance to any wicked plot.

I begged him to understand that I knew right well he would do no manner of wrong to any man, and asked the privilege of being with him all the time, to serve him when he could not serve himself because of the irons that fettered his legs.

And so it was that I had opportunity to do that which made my master as true a friend as ever lad had, for in the later days when we were come to Virginia and beset by savages more cruel than wild beasts, he ventured his own life again and again to save mine, which was so worthless as compared with his.

Only that I might tell how the voyage progressed, did I go on deck, or have speech with Nathaniel Peacock, and only through me did my master know when we were come to this island or that, together with what was to be seen in such places.

SEVERAL ISLANDS VISITED

THEREFORE IT WAS THAT WHEN, on the next day after he was made a prisoner, we were come to anchor off that island which the savages called Gaudaloupe, and Nathaniel had been permitted to go on shore in one of the boats, I could tell my master of the wondrous waters which were found there.

Nathaniel told me that water spouted up out of the earth so hot, that when Captain Newport threw into it a piece of pork tied to a rope, the meat was cooked in half an hour, even as if it had been over a roaring hot fire.

After that we passed many islands, the names of which I could not discover, until we came to anchor within half a musket-shot from the shore of that land which is known as Nevis. Here we lay six days, and the chief men of the company went on shore for sport and to hunt, save always either Captain Martin or Captain Kendall, who remained on board to watch the poor prisoner, while he, my master, lay in his narrow bed sweltering under the great heat.

During all this while, the seamen and our gentlemen got much profit and sport from hunting and fishing, adding in no small degree to our store of food. Had Captain Smith not been kept from going on shore by the wickedness of those who were jealous because of his great fame as a soldier, I dare venture to say our stay at this island of Nevis would have been far more to our advantage.

From this place we went to what Master Hunt told me were the Virgin Islands, and here the men went ashore again to hunt; but my master, speaking no harsh words against those who were wronging him, lay in the small, stinging hot room, unable to get for himself even a cup of water, though I took good care he should not suffer from lack of kindly care.

Then on a certain day we sailed past that land which Captain Gosnold told me was Porto Rico, and next morning came to anchor off the island of Mona, where the seamen were sent ashore to get fresh water, for our supply was running low.

Captain Newport, and many of the other gentlemen, went on shore to hunt, and so great was the heat that Master Edward Brookes fell down dead, one of the sailors telling Nathaniel that the poor

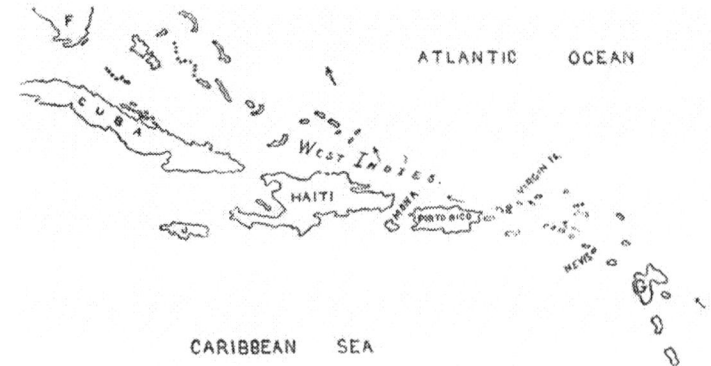

man's fat was melted until he could no longer live; but Captain Smith, who knows more concerning such matters than all this company rolled into one, save I might except Master Hunt, declared that the fat of a live person does not melt, however great the heat. It is the sun shining too fiercely on one's head that brings about death, and thus it was that Master Brookes died.

A VARIETY OF WILD GAME

OUR GENTLEMEN WHO HAD THE HEART to make prisoner of so honest, upright a man as my master, did not cease their sport because of what had befallen Master Brookes, but continued at the hunting until they had brought down two wild boars and also an animal fashioned like unto nothing I had ever seen before. It was something after the manner of a serpent, but speckled on the stomach as is a toad, and Captain Smith believed the true name of it to be Iguana, the like of which he says that he has often seen in other countries and that its flesh makes very good eating.

If any one save Captain Smith had said this, I should have found it hard to believe him, and as it was I was glad my belief was not put to the test.

Two days afterward we were come to an island which Master Hunt says is known to seamen as Monica, and there it was that Nathaniel went on shore in one of the boats, coming back at night to tell me a most wondrous story.

He declared that the birds and their eggs were so plentiful that the whole island was covered with them; that one could not set down his foot, save upon eggs, or birds sitting on their nests, some of which could hardly be driven away even with blows, and when they rose in the air, the noise made by their wings was so great as to deafen a person.

Our seamen loaded two boats full of the eggs in three hours, and all in the fleet feasted for several days on such as had not yet been spoiled by the warmth of the birds' bodies.

It was on the next day that we left behind us those islands which Captain Smith told me were the West Indies, and the seaman who stood at the helm when I came on deck to get water for my master, said we were steering a northerly course, which would soon bring us to the land of Virginia.

THE TEMPEST

On that very night, however, such a tempest of wind and of rain came upon us that I was not the only one who believed the *Susan Constant* must be crushed like an eggshell under the great mountains of water which at times rolled completely over her, so flooding the decks that but few could venture out to do whatsoever of work was needed to keep the ship afloat.

After this fierce tempest, when the Lord permitted that even our pinnace should ride in safety, it was believed that we were come near to the new world, and by day and by night the seamen stood at the rail, throwing the lead every few minutes in order to discover if we were venturing into shoal water.

Nathaniel and I used to stand by watching them, and wishing that we might be allowed to throw the line, but never quite getting up our courage to say so, knowing full well we should probably make a tangle of it.

THE NEW COUNTRY SIGHTED

As Master George Percy has set down in the writings which I have copied for him since we came to Virginia, it was on the twenty-sixth day of April, in the year of our Lord 1607, at about four o'clock in the morning, when we were come within sight of that land where were to be built homes, not only for our company of one hundred and five, counting the boys, but for all who should come after us.

It was while the ship lay off the land, her decks crowded with our company who fain would get the first clear view of that country in which they were to live, if the savages permitted, that I asked my master who among the gentlemen of the cabin was the leader in this adventure.

To my surprise, he told me that it was not yet known. The London Company had made an election of those among the gentlemen who should form the new government, and had written down the names, together with instructions as to what should be done; but this writing was enclosed in a box which was not to be opened until we had come to the end of our voyage.

THE LEADER NOT KNOWN

There could be no doubt but that Captain Kendall and Captain Martin both believed that when the will of the London Company was made known, it would be found they stood in high command; but there was in my heart a great hope that my master might have been named.

Yet when I put the matter to him in so many words, he treated the matter lightly, saying it could hardly be, else they had not dared to treat him thus shamefully.

However, it was soon to be known, if the commands of the London Company were obeyed, for now we had come to this new land of Virginia, and the time was near at hand when would be opened the box containing the names of those who were to be officers in the town we hoped soon to build.

As for myself, I was so excited it seemed impossible to remain quiet many seconds in one place, and I fear that my duties, which consisted only in waiting upon the prisoner, my master, were sadly neglected because of the anxiety in my mind to know who the merchants in London had named as rulers of the settlement about to be made in the new world.

One would have believed from Captain Smith's manner that he had no concern whatsoever as to the result of all this wickedness and scheming, for it was neither more nor less than such, as I looked at the matter, on the part of Captain Kendall and Captain Martin.

Here we were in sight of the new world, at a place where we were to live all the remainder of our lives, and he a prisoner in chains; but yet never a word of complaint came from his lips.

ARRIVAL AT CHESAPEAKE BAY

When the day had fully dawned, and the fleet stood in toward the noble bay, between two capes, which were afterward named Cape Henry and Cape Comfort, Captain Smith directed me to go on deck, in order to keep him informed of what might be happening.

He told me there was no question in his mind but that we were come to the mouth of Chesapeake Bay, where it had been agreed with the London merchants we were to go on shore.

Standing at the head of the companionway, but not venturing out on deck lest I should be sent to some other part of the ship, and thus be unable to give my master the information which he desired, I looked out upon what seemed to me the most goodly land that could be found in all the wide world.

Trees there were of size fit for masts to the king's ships; flowers bordered the shore until there were seemingly great waves of this color, or of that, as far as eye could reach, and set within this dazzling array of green and gold, and of red and yellow, was a great sea, which Captain Smith said was called the Chesapeake Bay.

We entered for some distance, mayhap three or four miles, before coming to anchor, and then Master Wingfield, Captain Gosnold, and Captain Newport went on shore with a party of thirty, made up of seamen and gentlemen, and my master, who had not so much as stretched his legs since we sailed from Martinique, was left in his narrow cabin with none but me to care for him!

I had thought they would open the box containing the instructions from London, before doing anything else; but Captain Smith was of the mind that such business could wait until they had explored sufficiently to find a place where the new town might be built.

It was a long, weary, anxious day for me. The party had left the ship in the morning, remaining absent until nightfall, and at least four or five times every hour did I run up from the cabin to gaze shoreward in the hope of seeing them return, for I was most eager to have the business pushed forward, and to know whether my master's enemies were given, by the London Company, permission to do whatsoever they pleased.

AN ATTACK BY THE SAVAGES

Just after sunset, and before the darkness of night closed in, those who had been on shore came back very hurriedly and in disorder, bringing with them in the foremost boat, two wounded men.

"They have had a battle with some one, Master," I reported, before yet the boats were come alongside, and for the first time that day did Captain Smith appear to be deeply concerned. I heard him say as if to himself, not intending that the words should reach me:

"Lack of caution in dealing with the savages is like to cost us dearly."

Half an hour later I heard all the story from Nathaniel Peacock, who had believed himself fortunate when he was allowed to accompany the party on shore.

According to his account, the company from the fleet roamed over much of the land during the day, finding fair meadows and goodly trees, with streams of fresh water here and there bespeaking fish in abundance.

Nothing was seen or heard to disturb our people until the signal had been given for all to go on board the boats, that they might return to the ships, and then it was that a number of naked, brown men, creeping upon their hands and knees like animals, with bows and arrows held between their teeth, came out suddenly from amid the foliage to the number, as Nathaniel declared, of not less than an hundred.

While the white men stood dismayed, awaiting some order from those who chose to call themselves leaders, the savages shot a multitude of arrows into the midst of the company, wounding Captain Gabriel Archer in both his hands, and dangerously hurting one of the seamen.

Captain Gosnold gave command for the firearms to be discharged, whereupon the savages disappeared suddenly, and without delay our people returned to the fleet.

READING THE LONDON COMPANY'S ORDERS

An hour later, when those who had just come from the shore had been refreshed with food, I noted with much of anxiety that all the gentlemen of the company, not only such as belonged on board the *Susan Constant*, but those from the *Speedwell*, gathered in the great cabin of our ship, and, looking out ever so cautiously, while the door of Captain Smith's room was ajar, I saw them gather around the big table on which, as if it were something of greatest value, was placed a box made of some dark colored wood.

It was Master Hunt who opened this, and, taking out a paper, he read in a voice so loud that even my master, as he lay in his narrow bed, could hear the names of those who were chosen by the London Company to form the Council for the government of the new land of Virginia.

These are the names as he read them: Bartholomew Gosnold, Edward Wingfield, Christopher Newport, John Smith, John Ratcliffe, John Martin and George Kendall.

My heart seemingly leaped into my throat with triumph when I thus heard the name of my master among those who were to stand as leaders of the company, and so excited had I become that that which Master Hunt read from the remainder of the paper failed to attract my attention.

I learned afterward, however, that among the rules governing the actions of this Council, was one that a President should be chosen each year, and that matters of moment were to be determined by vote of the Council, in which the President might cast two ballots.

CAPTAIN SMITH A MEMBER OF THE COUNCIL

It was when Master Hunt ceased reading that I believed my master would be set free without delay, for of a verity he had the same right to take part in the deliberations as any other, since it was the will of the London Company that he should be one of the leaders; but much to my surprise nothing of the kind was done.

Captain Kendall, seeing the door of my master's room slightly open, arose from the table and closed it, as if he were about to say something which should not be heard by Captain Smith.

I would have opened the door again, but that my master bade me leave it closed, and when an hour or more had passed, Master Hunt came in to us, stating that it had not yet been decided by the other members of the Council whether Captain Smith should be allowed to take part in the affairs, as the London Company had decided, or whether he should be sent home for judgment when the fleet returned. But meanwhile he was to have his liberty.

Then it was that Master Hunt, talking like the true man he ever showed himself to be, advised Captain Smith to do in all things, so far as the other members of the Council permitted, as if nothing had gone awry, claiming that before we had been many days in this land, those who had brought charges against him would fail of making them good.

Had I been the one thus so grievously injured, the whole company might have shipwrecked themselves before I would have raised a hand, all of which goes to show that I had not learned to rule my temper.

Captain Smith, however, agreed with all Master Hunt said, and then it was that I was sent forward once more. My master went on deck for the first time since we had left Martinique, walking to and fro swiftly, as if it pleased him to have command of his legs once more.

CAPTAIN SMITH FORCED TO REMAIN ABOARD

IF MASTER HUNT and Master Wingfield had been able to bring the others around to their way of thinking, Captain Smith would have taken his rightful place in the Council without delay. Instead of which, however, he remained on board the ship idle, when there was much that he could have done better than any other, from the day on which we came in sight of Virginia, which was the twenty-sixth day of April, until the fifthteenth day of June.

During all this time, those of the Council who were his enemies claimed that they could prove he had laid plans to murder all the chief men, and take his place as king; but yet they did not do so, and my master refused to hold any parley with them, except that he claimed he was innocent of all wrong in thought or in act.

When the others of the fleet set off to spy out the land, my master remained aboard the ship, still being a prisoner, except so far that he wore no fetters, and I would not have left him save he had commanded me sharply, for at that time, so sore was his heart, that even a lad like me could now and then say some word which might have in it somewhat of cheer.

During this time that Captain Smith was with the company and yet not numbered as one of them, the other gentlemen explored the country, and more than once was Nathaniel Peacock allowed to accompany them, therefore did I hear much which otherwise would not have been told me.

And what happened during these two months when the gentlemen were much the same as quarreling among themselves, I shall set down in as few words as possible, to the end that I may the sooner come to that story of our life in the new village, which some called James Fort, and others James Town, after King James of England.

EXPLORING THE COUNTRY

When the shallop had been taken out of the hold of the *Susan Constant*, and put together by the carpenters, our people explored the shores of the bay and the broad streams running into it, meeting with savages here and there, and holding some little converse with them. A few were found to be friendly, while others appeared to think we were stealing their land by thus coming among them.

One of the most friendly of the savages, so Nathaniel said, having shown by making marks on the ground with his foot that he wished to tell our people about the country, and having been given a pen and paper, drew a map of the river with great care, putting in the islands and waterfalls and mountains that our men would come to, and afterward he even brought food to our people such as wheat and little sweet nuts and berries.

I myself would have been pleased to go on shore and see these strange people, but not being able to do so save at the cost of leaving my master, I can only repeat some of the curious things which Nathaniel Peacock told me.

It must be known that there was more than one nation, or tribe, of savages in this new land of Virginia, and each had its king or chief, who was called the werowance. I might set down the names of these tribes, and yet it would be so much labor lost, because they are more like fanciful than real words. As, for example, there were the Paspaheghes, whose werowance was seemingly more friendly to our people than were the others.

Again, there were the Rapahannas, who wore the legs of birds through holes in their ears, and had all the hair on the right side of their heads shaven closely.

It gives them much pleasure to dance, so Nathaniel said, he having seen them jumping around more like so many wolves, rather than human beings, for the space of half an hour, shouting and singing all the while.

All the Indians smoked an herb called tobacco, which grows abundantly in this land, and I have Nathaniel's word for it that one savage had a tobacco pipe nearly a yard long, with the device of a deer carved at the great end of it big enough to dash out one's brains with.

There is very much more which might be said about these savages that would be of interest; but I am minded now to leave such stories for others to tell, and come to the day when Captain Newport was ready to sail with the *Susan Constant* and the *Goodspeed* back to England, for his share in the adventure was only to bring us over from England, after which he had agreed to return.

The pinnace was to be left behind for the use of us who remained in the strange land.

Before this time, meaning the thirteenth day of May, the members of the Council had decided upon the place where we were to build our village. It was to be in the country of the Paspahegh Indians, at a certain spot near the shore where the water runs so deep that our ships can lie moored to the trees in six fathoms.

THE PEOPLE LAND FROM THE SHIPS

THEN IT WAS THAT ALL THE PEOPLE WENT ON SHORE, some to set up the tents of cloth which we had brought with us to serve as shelters before houses could be built; others to lay out a fort, which it was needed should be made as early as possible because of the savages, and yet a certain other number being told off to stand guard against the brown men, who had already shown that they could be most dangerous enemies.

My master went ashore, as a matter of course, with the others, I sticking close to his side; but neither of us taking any part in the work which had been begun, because the charges of wickedness were still hanging over his head.

Had Captain Smith been allowed a voice in the Council, certain it is he never would have chosen this place in which to make the town, for he pointed out to me that the land lay so low that when the river was at its height the dampness must be great, and, therefore, exceeding unhealthful, while there was back of it such an extent of forest, as made it most difficult to defend, in case the savages came against us.

Captain Smith aided me in building for ourselves a hut in front of an overhanging rock, with the branches of trees. It was a poor shelter at the best; but he declared it would serve us until such time as he was given his rightful place among the people, or had been sent back a prisoner to England.

CAPTAIN SMITH PROVEN INNOCENT

THIS SERVED US AS A LIVING PLACE FOR MANY DAYS, or until my master was come into his own, as he did before the fort was finished, when, on one certain morning, he demanded of the other members of the Council that they put him on trial to learn whether the charges could be proven or not, and this was done on the day before Captain Newport was to take the ships back to England.

There is little need for me to say that Captain Kendall's stories of the plot, in which he said my master was concerned, came to naught. There were none to prove that he had ever spoken of such a matter, and the result of the trial was that they gave him his rightful place at the head of the company.

Before many months were passed, all came to know that but for him the white people in Jamestown would have come to their deaths.

WE WHO WERE LEFT BEHIND

It was on the fifteenth day of June when the ships sailed out of the Chesapeake Bay, leaving on the banks of the river we called the James, a hundred men and boys, all told, to hold their lives and their liberty against thousands upon thousands of naked savages, who had already shown that they desired to be enemies rather than friends.

Even in the eyes of a boy, it was an odd company to battle with the savages and the wilderness, for the greater number were

those who called themselves gentlemen, and who believed it beneath their station to do any labor whatsoever, therefore did it seem to me that this new town would be burdened sorely with so many drones.

Master Hunt, the preacher, could in good truth call himself a gentleman, and yet I myself saw him, within two hours after we were landed, nailing a piece of timber between two trees that he might stretch a square of sail-cloth over it, thus making what served as the first church in the country of Virginia.

Yet Captain Smith has said again and again, that the discourses of Master Hunt under that poor shelter of cloth, were, to his mind, more like the real praising of God, than any he had ever heard in the costly buildings of the old world.

For the better understanding of certain things which happened to us after we had begun to build the village of Jamestown, it should be remembered that of all the savages in the country roundabout, the most friendly were those who lived in the same settlement with Powhatan, who was, so Captain Smith said, the true head and king of all the Indians in Virginia.

BAKING BREAD WITHOUT OVENS

IT WAS IN THIS TOWN OF POWHATAN'S that I discovered how to bake bread without an oven or other fire than what might be built on the open ground, and it was well I had my eyes open at that time, otherwise Captain Smith and I had gone supperless to bed again and again, for there were many days when our stomachs cried painfully because of emptiness.

While my master was talking with the king, Powhatan, on matters concerning affairs at Jamestown, I saw an Indian girl, whose name I afterward came to know was Pocahontas, making bread, and observed her carefully. She had white meal, but whether of barley, or the wheat called Indian corn, or Guinny wheat I could not say, and this she mixed into a paste with hot water; making it of such thickness that it could easily be rolled into little balls or cakes.

After the mixture had been thus shaped, she dropped the balls into a pot of boiling water, letting them stay there until well soaked, when she laid them on a smooth stone in front of the fire until they had hardened and browned like unto bread that has been cooked in the oven.

But I have set myself to the task of telling how we of Jamestown lived during that time when my master was much the same as the head of the government, and it is not well to begin the story with bread making.

AN UNEQUAL DIVISION OF LABOR

FIRST I MUST EXPLAIN UPON WHAT TERMS these people, the greater number of whom called themselves gentlemen, and therefore claimed to be ashamed to labor with their hands, had come together under control of those merchants in London, who were known as the London Company.

No person in the town of James was allowed to own any land except as he had his share of the whole. Everyone was expected to work for the good of the village, and whatsoever of crops was raised, belonged to all the people. It was not permitted that the more industrious should plant the land and claim that which grew under their toil.

Ours was supposed to be one big family, with each laboring to help the others at the same time he helped himself, and the result was that those who worked only a single hour each day, had as much of the general stores as he who remained in the field from morning until night.

Although my master had agreed to this plan before the fleet sailed from England, he soon came to understand that it was not the best for a new land, where it was needed that each person should labor to the utmost of his powers.

The London Company had provided a certain number of tents made of cloth, which were supposed to be enough to give shelter to all the people, and yet, because those who had charge of the matter had made a mistake, through ignorance or for the sake of gain, there were no more than would provide for the members of the Council, who appeared to think they should be lodged in better fashion than those who were not in authority.

My master could well have laid claim to one of these cloth houses; but because of the charges which had been made against him by Captain Kendall and Captain Martin, the sting of which yet remained, he chose to live by himself. Thus it was that he and I threw up the roof of branches concerning which I have spoken; but it was only to shelter us until better could be built.

BUILDING A HOUSE OF LOGS

While the others were hunting here and there for the gold which it had been said could be picked up in Virginia as one gathers acorns in the old world, Captain Smith set about making a house of logs such as would protect him from the storms of winter as well as from the summer sun.

This he did by laying four logs on the ground in the form of a square, and so cutting notches in the ends of each that when it was

placed on the top of another, and at right angles with it, the hewn portions would interlock, one with the other, holding all firmly in place. On top of these, other huge tree trunks were laid with the same notching of the ends.

It was a vast amount of labor, thus to roll up the heavy logs in the form of a square until a pen or box had been made as high as a man's head, and then over that was built a roof of logs fastened together with wooden pins, or pegs, for iron nails were all too scarce and costly to be used for such purpose.

When the house had been built thus far, the roof was formed of no more than four or five logs on which a thatching of grass was to be laid later, and the ends, in what might be called the "peak of the roof," were open to the weather. Then it was that roughly hewn planks, or logs split into three or four strips, called puncheons, were pegged with wooden nails on the sides, or ends, where doors or windows were to be made.

Then the space inside this framework was sawed out, and behold you had a doorway, or the opening for a window, to be filled in afterward as time and material with which to work might permit.

After this had been done, the ends under the roof were covered with yet more logs, sawn to the proper length and pegged together, until, save for the crevices between the timbers, the whole gave protection against the weather.

Then came the work of thatching the roof, which was done by the branches of trees, dried grass, or bark. My master put on first a layer of branches from which the leaves had been stripped, and over that we laid coarse grass to the depth of six or eight inches, binding the same down with small saplings running from one side to the other, to the number of ten on each slope of the roof. To me was given the task of closing up the crevices between the logs with mud and grass mixed, and this I did the better because Nathaniel Peacock worked with me, doing his full share of the labor.

KEEPING HOUSE

WHEN WE CAME ASHORE FROM THE SHIPS, no one claimed Nathaniel as servant, and he, burning to be in my company, asked Captain Smith's permission to enter his employ. My master replied that it had not been in his mind there should be servants and lords in this new world of Virginia, where one was supposed to be on the same footing as another; but if Nathaniel were minded to live under the same roof with us, and would cheerfully perform his full share of the labor, it might be as he desired.

Because our house was the first to be put up in the new village, and, being made of logs, was by far the best shelter, even in comparison with the tents of cloth, Nathaniel and I decided that it should be the most homelike, if indeed that could be compassed where were no women to keep things cleanly.

I am in doubt as to whether Captain Smith, great traveler and brave adventurer though he was, had even realized that with only men to perform the household duties, there would be much lack of comfort.

The floor of the house was only the bare earth beaten down hard. We lads made brooms, by tying the twigs of trees to a stick, which was not what might be called a good makeshift, and yet with such we kept the inside of our home far more cleanly than were some of the tents.

LACK OF CLEANLINESS IN THE VILLAGE

THERE WERE MANY WHO BELIEVED, because there were no women in our midst, we should spare our labor in the way of keeping cleanly, and before we had been in the new village a week, the floors of many of the dwellings were littered with dirt of various kinds, until that which should have been a home, looked more like a place in which swine are kept.

From the very first day we came ashore, good Master Hunt went about urging that great effort be made to keep the houses, and the paths around them, cleanly, saying that unless we did so, there was like to be a plague of sickness come among us. With some his preaching did good, but by far the greater number, and these chiefly to be found among the self-called gentlemen, gave no heed.

It was as if these lazy ones delighted in filth. Again and again have I seen one or another throw the scrapings of the trencher bowls just outside the door of the tent or hut, where those who came or went must of a necessity tread upon them, and one need not struggle hard to realize what soon was the condition of the village.

After a heavy shower many of the paths were covered ankle deep with filth of all kinds, and when the sun shone warm and bright, the stench was too horrible to be described by ordinary words.

CAVE HOMES

THERE WERE OTHER KINDS OF HOMES, and quite a number of them, that were made neither of cloth nor of logs. These were holes dug in the side of small hillocks until a sleeping room had been made, when the front part was covered with brush or logs, built outward from the hill to form a kitchen.

During a storm these cave homes were damp, often times actually muddy, and those who slept therein were but inviting the mortal sickness that came all too soon among us, until it was as if the Angel of Death had taken possession of Jamestown.

Captain Smith said everything he could to persuade these people, who were content to live in a hole in the ground, that they were little better than beasts of the field.

But so long as the foolish ones continued to believe this new world was much the same as filled with gold and silver, so long they wasted their time searching.

THE GOLDEN FEVER

BUT FOR THIS GOLDEN FEVER, which attacked the gentlemen more fiercely than it did the common people, the story of Jamestown would not have been one of disaster brought about by willful heedlessness and stupidity.

Again and again did Captain Smith urge that crops be planted, while it was yet time, in order that there might be food at hand when the winter came; but he had not yet been allowed to take his place in the Council, and those who had the thirst for gold strong upon them, taunted him with the fact that he had no right to raise his voice above the meanest of the company. They refused to listen when he would have spoken with them as a friend, and laughed him to scorn when he begged that they take heed to their own lives.

I cannot understand why our people were so crazy. Even though Nathaniel and I were but lads, with no experience of adventure such as was before us, we could realize that unless a man plants he may not reap, and because we had been hungry many a time in London town, we knew full well that when the season had passed there was like to be a famine among us.

I can well understand, now that I am a man grown, why our people were so careless regarding the future, for everywhere around us was food in plenty. Huge flocks of wild swans circled above our heads, trumpeting the warning that winter would come before gold could be found. Wild geese, cleaving the air in wedge-shaped line, honked harshly that the season for gathering stores of food was passing, while at times, on a dull morning, it was as if the waters of the bay were covered completely with ducks of many kinds.

DUCKS AND OYSTERS

I HAVE HEARD CAPTAIN SMITH SAY MORE THAN ONCE, that he had seen flocks of ducks a full mile wide and five or six miles long, wherein canvasbacks, mallard, widgeon, redheads, dottrel, sheldrake, and teal swam wing to wing, actually crowding each other. When such flocks rose in the air, the noise made by their wings was like unto the roaring of a tempest at sea.

Then there was bed after bed of oysters, many of which were uncovered at ebb tide, when a hungry man might stand and eat his fill of shellfish, never one of them less than six inches long, and many twice that size.

It is little wonder that the gold crazed men refused to listen while my master warned them that the day might come when they would be hungry to the verge of starvation.

Now perhaps you will like to hear how we two lads, bred in London town, with never a care as to how our food had been cooked, so that we had enough with which to fill our stomachs, made shift

to prepare meals that could be eaten by Captain Smith, for so we did after taking counsel with the girl Pocahontas from Powhatan's village.

ROASTING OYSTERS

IN THE FIRST PLACE, THE SHELL FISH CALLED OYSTERS are readily cooked, or may be eaten raw with great satisfaction. I know not what our people of Virginia would have done without them, and yet it was only by chance or accident that we came to learn how nourishing they are.

A company of our gentlemen had set off to explore the country very shortly after we came ashore from the fleet, and while going through that portion of the forest which borders upon the bay, happened upon four savages who were cooking something over the fire.

The Indians ran away in alarm, and, on coming up to discover what the brown men had which was good to eat, the explorers found a large number of oysters roasting on the coals. Through curiosity, one of our gentlemen tasted of the fish, and, much to his surprise, found it very agreeable to the stomach.

Before telling his companions the result of his experiment, he ate all the oysters that had been cooked, which were more than two dozen large ones, and then, instead of exploring the land any further on that day, our gentlemen spent their time gathering and roasting the very agreeable fish.

As a matter of course, the news of this discovery spread throughout the settlement, and straightway every person was eating oysters; but they soon tired of them, hankering after wheat of some kind.

Among those who served some of the gentlemen even as Nathaniel and I aimed to serve Captain Smith, was James Brumfield, a lazy, shiftless lad near to seventeen years old. Being hungry, and not inclined to build a fire, because it would be necessary to gather fuel, he ventured to taste of a raw oyster. Finding it pleasant to the mouth, he actually gorged himself until sickness put an end to the gluttonous meal.

It can thus be seen that even though Nathaniel and I had never been apprenticed to a cook, it was not difficult for us to serve our master with oysters roasted or raw, laid on that which answered in the stead of a table, in their own shells.

LEARNING TO COOK OTHER THINGS

Then again the Indian girl had shown us how to boil beans, peas, Indian corn, and pumpkins together, making a kind of porridge which is most pleasant, and affords a welcome change from oysters; but the great drawback is that we are not able to come at the various things needed for the making of it, except when our gentlemen have been fortunate in trading with the brown men, which is not often.

This Indian corn, pounded and boiled until soft, is a dish

Captain Smith eats of with an appetite, provided it is well salted, and one does not need to be a king's cook in order to make it ready for the table. The pounding is the hardest and most difficult portion of the task, for the kernels are exceeding flinty, and fly off at a great distance when struck a glancing blow.

Nathaniel and I have brought inside our house a large, flat rock, on which we pound the corn, and one of us is kept busy picking up the grains that fly here and there as if possessed of an evil spirit. Newsamp is the name which the savages give to this cooking of wheat.

I have an idea that when we get a mill for grinding, it will be possible to break the kernels easily and quickly between the millstones, without crushing a goodly portion of them to meal.

When the Indian corn is young, that is to say, before it has grown hard, the ears as plucked from the stalks may be roasted before the coals with great profit, and when we would give our master something unusually pleasing, Nathaniel and I go abroad in search of the gardens made by the savages, where we may get, by bargaining, a supply of roasting ears.

With a trencher of porridge, and a dozen roasting ears, together with a half score of the bread balls such as I have already written about, Captain Smith can satisfy his hunger with great pleasure, and then it is that he declares he has the most comfortable home in all Virginia, thanks to his "houseboys," as he is pleased to call us.

THE SWEET POTATO ROOT

The Indians have roots, which some of our gentlemen call sweet potatoes, which are by no means unpleasant to the taste, the only difficulty being that we cannot get any great quantity of them. Our master declares that when we make a garden, this root shall be the first thing planted, and after it has ripened, we will have some cooked every day.

Nathaniel and I have no trouble in preparing the root, for it may be roasted in the ashes, boiled into a pudding which should be well salted, or mixed with the meal of Indian corn and made into a kind of sweet cake.

However, we lads have not had good success in baking this last dish, because of the ashes which fly out of the fire when the wind blows ever so slightly. Captain Smith declares that he would rather have the ashes without the meal and sweet potato, if indeed he must eat any, but of course when he speaks thus, it is only in the way of making sport.

Captain Kendall, who, because he has made two voyages to the Indies, believes himself a wondrously wise man, says that he who eats sweet potatoes at least once each day will not live above seven years, and he who eats them twice every day will become blind, after which all his teeth will drop out.

Because of this prediction, many of our gentlemen are not willing even so much as to taste of the root, but Captain Smith says that wise men may grow fat where fools starve, therefore he gathers up all the sweet potatoes which the others have thrown away, for they please him exceeding well.

A TOUCH OF HOMESICKNESS

There is no need for me to say that it makes both Nathaniel and me glad to be praised by our master, because we keep the house cleanly and strive to serve the food in such a manner as not to offend the eye; but we would willingly dispense with such welcome words if thereby it would be possible to see a woman messing around the place.

Strive as boys may, they cannot attend to household matters as do girls or women, who have been brought into the world knowing how to perform such tasks, and it is more homelike to see them around.

Nathaniel and I often picture to each other what this village of Jamestown would be if in each camp, cave, or log hut a woman was in command, and ever when we talk thus comes into my heart a sickness for the old homes of England, even though after my mother died there was none for me; but yet it would do me a world of good even to look upon a housewife.

A most friendly gentleman is Master Hunt, and even though he is so far above me in station, I never fail of getting a kindly greeting when I am so fortunate as to meet him. He comes often to see Captain Smith, for the two talk long and earnestly over the matter of the Council, and at such times it is as if he went out of his way to give me a good word.

MASTER HUNT'S PREACHING

THEREFORE IT IS THAT I GO TO HEAR HIM PREACH whenever the people are summoned to a meeting beneath the square of canvas in the wood, and more than once I have heard from him that which has taken the sickness for home out of my heart. Our people are not inclined to listen to him in great numbers, however. I have never seen above twenty at one time, the others being busy in the search for gold, or trying to decide among themselves as to how it may best be found.

More than once have I heard Master Hunt say, while talking privately with my master, that there would be greater hope for this village of ours if we had more laborers and less gentlemen, for in a new land it is only work that can win in the battle against the savages and the wilderness.

Four carpenters, one blacksmith, two bricklayers, a mason, a sailor, a barber, a tailor, and a drummer make up the list of skilled workmen, if, indeed, one who can do nothing save drum may be called a laborer. To these may be added twelve serving men and four

boys. All the others are gentlemen, or, as Master Hunt puts it, drones expecting to live through the mercy of God whom they turn their backs upon.

NEGLECTING TO PROVIDE FOR THE FUTURE

The one thing which seemed most surprising to us lads, after Captain Smith had called it to our notice, was that these people, who knew there could be no question but that the winter would find them in Jamestown, when there could be neither roasting ears, peas, beans, nor fowls of the air to be come at, made no provision for a harvest.

Captain Smith, not being allowed to raise his voice in the Council, could only speak as one whose words have little weight, since he was not in authority; but he lost no opportunity of telling these gold seekers that only those who sowed might reap, and unless seed was put into the ground, there would be no crops to serve as food during the winter.

Even Master Wingfield, the President of the Council, refused to listen when my master would have spoken to him as a friend. He gave more heed to exploring the land, than to what might be our fate in the future. He would not even allow the gentlemen to make such a fort as might withstand an assault by the savages, seeming to think it of more importance to know what was to be found on the banks of this river or of that, than to guard against those brown people who daily gave token of being unfriendly.

The serving men and laborers were employed in making clapboards that we might have a cargo with which to fill one of Captain Newport's ships when he returned from England, according to the plans of the London Company. The gentlemen roamed here or there, seeking the yellow metal which had much the same as caused a madness among them; and, save in the case of Master Hunt and Captain Smith, none planted even the smallest garden.

SURPRISED BY SAVAGES

The fort, as it was called, had been built only of the branches of trees, and might easily have been overrun by savages bent on doing us harm.

It was while Master Wingfield, with thirty of the gentlemen, was gone to visit Powhatan's village, and the others were hunting for gold, leaving only my master and the preacher to look after the serving men and the laborers, that upward of an hundred naked savages suddenly came down upon us, counting to make an end of all who were in the town.

It was a most fearsome sight to see the brown men, their bodies painted with many colors, carrying bows and arrows, dash out from among the trees bent on taking our lives, and for what seemed a very long while our people ran here and there like ants whose nest has been broken in upon.

Captain Smith gave no heed to his own safety; but

shouted for all to take refuge in our house of logs, while Master Hunt did what he might to aid in the defence; yet, because there had been no exercise at arms, nor training, that each should know what was his part at such a time, seventeen of the people were wounded, some grievously, and one boy, James Brumfield of whom I have already spoken, was killed by an arrow piercing his eye.

STRENGTHENING THE FORT

Next day, when Master Wingfield and his following came in, none the better for having gone to Powhatan's village, all understood that it would have been wiser had they listened to my master when he counseled them to take exercise at arms, and straightway all the men were set about making a fort with a palisade, which last is the name for a fence built of logs set on end, side by side, in the ground, and rising so high that the enemy may not climb over it.

This work took all the time of the laborers until the summer was gone, and in the meanwhile the gentlemen made use of the stores left us by the fleet, until there remained no more than one half pint of wheat to each man for a day's food.

The savages strove by day and by night to murder us, till it was no longer safe to go in search of oysters or wildfowl, and from wheat which had lain so long in the holds of the ships that nearly every grain in it had a worm, did we get our only nourishment.

The labor of building the palisade was most grievous, and it was not within the power of man to continue it while eating such food; therefore the sickness came upon us, when it was as if all had been condemned to die.

A TIME OF SICKNESS AND DEATH

The first who went out from among us, was John Asbie, on the sixth of August. Three days later George Flowers followed him. On the tenth of the same month William Bruster, one of the gentlemen, died of a wound given by the savages while he was searching for gold, and two others laid down their lives within the next eight and forty hours.

Then the deaths came rapidly, gentlemen as well as serving men or laborers, until near eighty of our company were either in the grave, or unable to move out of such shelters as served as houses.

A great fear came upon all, save that my master held his head as high as ever, and went here and there with Master Hunt to do what he might toward soothing the sick and comforting the dying.

It was on the twentieth day of August when Captain Bartholomew Gosnold, one of the Council, died, and then Master Wingfield forgot all else save his own safety. More than one in our village declared that he was making ready the pinnace that he might run away from us, as if the Angel of Death could be escaped from by flight.

It was starvation brought about by sheer neglect, together with lying upon the bare ground and drinking of the river water, which by this time was very muddy, that had brought us to such a pass.

Save for the king, Powhatan, and some few of the other savages in authority, we must all have died; but when there were only five in all our company able to stand without aid, God touched the hearts of these Indians.

They, who had lately been trying to kill us, suddenly came to do what they might toward saving our lives after a full half of the company were in the grave. They brought food such as was needed to nourish us, and within a short time the greater number of us who were left alive, could go about, but only with difficulty.

It was a time of terror, of suffering, and of close acquaintance with death such as I cannot set down in words, for even at this late day the thought of what we then endured chills my heart.

When we had been restored to health and strength, and were no longer hungry, thanks to those who had been our bitter enemies, the chief men of the village began to realize that my master had not only given good advice on all occasions, but stood among them bravely when the President of the Council was making preparations to run away.

CAPTAIN SMITH GAINS AUTHORITY

THERE WAS BUT LITTLE IDLE talk made by the members of the Council in deciding that Master Wingfield should be deprived of his office, and Master Ratcliffe set in his place.

Captain Smith was called upon to take his proper position in the government, and, what was more, to him they gave the direction of all matters outside the town, which was much the

same as putting him in authority over even the President himself.

It was greatly to my pleasure that Captain Smith lost no time in exercising the power which had been given him. Nor was he at all gentle in dealing with those men who disdained to soil their hands by working, yet were willing to spend one day, and every day, searching for gold, without raising a finger toward adding to the general store, but at the same time claiming the right to have so much of food as would not only satisfy their hunger, but minister to their gluttony.

Nathaniel and I heard our master talking over the matter with the preacher, on the night the Council had given him full charge of everything save the dealings which might be had later with the London Company, therefore it was that we knew there would be different doings on the morrow.

Greatly did we rejoice thereat, for Jamestown had become as slovenly and ill-kempt a village as ever the sun shone upon.

Now it must be set down that these gentlemen of ours, when not searching for gold, were wont to play at bowls in the lanes and paths, that they might have amusement while the others were working, and

woe betide the serving man or laborer, who by accident interfered with their sports.

On this day, after the conversation with Master Hunt, all was changed. Captain Smith began his duties as guardian and director of the village by causing it to be proclaimed through the mouth of Nicholas Skot, our drummer, that there would be no more playing at bowls in the streets of Jamestown while it was necessary that very much work should be performed, and this spoken notice also stated, that whosoever dared to disobey the command should straightway be clapped into the stocks.

DISAGREEABLE MEASURES OF DISCIPLINE

Lest there should be any question as to whether my master intended to carry out this threat or no, William Laxon, one of the carpenters, was forthwith set to work building stocks in front of the tent where lived Master Ratcliffe, the new President of the Council. Nor was this the only change disagreeable to our gentlemen, which Captain Smith brought about. No sooner had Nicholas Skot proclaimed the order that whosoever played at bowls should be set in the stocks, than he was commanded to turn about and announce with all the strength of his lungs, so that every one in the village might hear and understand, that those who would not work should not have whatsoever to eat.

Verily this was a hard blow to the gentlemen of our company, who prided themselves upon never having done with their hands that which was useful.

One would have thought my master had made this rule for his own particular pleasure, for straightway those of the gentlemen who could least hold their tempers in check, gathered in the tent which Master Wingfield had taken for his own, and there agreed among themselves that if Captain Smith persisted in such brutal rule, they would overturn all the authority in the town, and end by setting the Captain himself in the stocks which William Laxon was then making.

It so chanced that Master Hunt overheard these threats at the time they were made, and, like a true friend and good citizen, reported the same to Captain Smith.

Whereupon my master chose a certain number from among those of the gentlemen who had become convinced that sharp measures were necessary if we of Jamestown would live throughout the winter, commanding that they make careful search of every tent, cave, hut or house in the village, taking therefrom all that was eatable, and storing it in the log house which had been put up for the common use.

Then he appointed Kellam Throgmorton, a gentleman who was well able to hold his own against any who might attempt to oppose him, to the office of guardian of the food, giving strict orders that nothing whatsoever which could be eaten, should be given to those who did not present good proof of having done a full day's labor.

Of course the people who lay sick were excused from such order, and Master Hunt was chosen to make up a list of those who must be fed, yet who were not able to work by reason of illness.

SIGNS OF REBELLION

NOW IT CAN WELL BE UNDERSTOOD that such measures as these caused no little in the way of rebellion, and during the two hours Nicholas Skot cried the proclamation through the streets and lanes of the village, the gentlemen who had determined to resist Captain Smith were in a fine state of ferment.

It was as if a company of crazy men had been suddenly let loose among us. Not content with plotting secretly against my master, they must needs swagger about, advising others to join them in their rebellion, and everywhere could be heard oaths and threats, in such language as was like to cause honest men's hair to stand on end.

For a short time Nathaniel Peacock and I actually trembled with fear, believing the house of logs would be pulled down over our heads, for no less than a dozen of the so called gentlemen were raging and storming outside; but disturbing Captain Smith not one whit. He sat there, furbishing his matchlock as if having nothing better with which to occupy the time; but, as can well be fancied, drinking in every word of mutiny which was uttered.

Then, as if he would saunter out for a stroll, the captain left the house, which was much the same as inviting these disorderly ones to attack him; but they lacked the courage, for he went to the fort without being molested.

THE SECOND PROCLAMATION

It seemed to me as if no more than half an hour had passed before Nicholas Skot was making another proclamation, and this time to the effect that whosoever, after that moment, was heard uttering profane words, should have a can full of cold water poured down his sleeve.

On hearing this, the unruly ones laughed in derision and straightway began to shout forth such a volley of oaths as I had never heard during a drunken brawl in the streets of London.

It was not long, however, that they were thus allowed to shame decent people. Down from the fort came Captain Smith, with six stout men behind him, and in a twinkling there was as hot a fight within twenty paces of Master Ratcliffe's tent, as could be well imagined.

And the result of it all was, much to the satisfaction of Nathaniel and myself, that every one of these men who had amused themselves by uttering the vilest of oaths, had a full can of the coldest water that could be procured, poured down the sleeve of his doublet.

The method of doing it was comical, if one could forget how serious was the situation. Two of my master's followers would pounce upon the fellow who was making the air blue with oaths, and, throwing him to the ground, hold him there firmly while the third raised his arm and carefully poured the water down the sleeve.

Now you may fancy that this was not very harsh treatment; but I afterward heard those who had been thus punished, say that they would choose five or six stout lashes on their backs, rather than take again such a dose as was dealt out on that day after John Smith was made captain and commander, or whatsoever you choose to call his office, in the village of Jamestown.

BUILDING A FORTIFIED VILLAGE

THERE IS LITTLE NEED FOR ME TO SAY that these were not the only reforms which my master brought about, after having waited long enough for our lazy gentlemen to understand that unless they set their hands to labor they could not eat from the general store.

He straightway set these idle ones to work building houses, declaring that if the sickness which had come among us was to be checked, our people must no longer sleep upon the ground, or in caves where the moisture gathered all around them.

He marked out places whereon log dwellings should be placed, in

such manner that when the houses had been set up, they would form a square, and, as I heard him tell Master Hunt, it was his intention to have all the buildings surrounded by a palisade in which should be many gates.

Thus, when all was finished, he would have a fort-like village, wherein the people could rest without fear of what the savages might be able to do.

By the time such work was well under way, and our gentlemen laboring as honest men should, after learning that it was necessary so to do unless they were willing to go hungry, Captain Smith set about adding to our store of food, for it was not to be supposed that we could depend for any length of time upon what the Indians might give us, and the winter would be long.

TRAPPING TURKEYS

THE WILD TURKEYS HAD appeared in the forest in great numbers, but few had been killed by our people because of the savages, many of whom were not to be trusted, even though the chiefs of three tribes professed to be friendly. It was this fact which had prevented us from doing much in the way of hunting.

Now that we were in such stress for food, and since all had turned laborers, whether willingly or no, much in the way of provisions was needed. Captain Smith set about taking the turkeys as he did about most other matters, which is to say, that it was done in a thorough manner.

Instead of being forced to spend at least one charge of powder for each fowl killed, he proposed that we trap them, and showed how it might be done, according to his belief.

Four men were told off to do the work, and they were kept busy cutting saplings and trimming them down until there was nothing

left save poles from fifteen to twenty feet long. Then, with these poles laid one above the other, a square pen was made, and at the top was a thatching of branches, so that no fowl larger than a pigeon might go through.

From one side of this trap, or turkey pen, was dug a ditch perhaps two feet deep, and the same in width, running straightway into the thicket where the turkeys were in the custom of roosting, for a distance of twenty feet or more. This ditch was carried underneath the side of the pen, where was an opening hardly more than large enough for one turkey to pass through. Corn was scattered along the whole length of the ditch, and thus was the trap set.

The turkeys, on finding the trail of corn, would follow hurriedly along, like the gluttons they are, with the idea of coming upon a larger hoard, and thus pass through into the pen. Once inside they were trapped securely, for the wild turkey holds his head so high that he can never see the way out through a hole which is at a level with his feet.

It was a most ingenious contrivance, and on the first morning after it had been set at night, we had fifty plump fellows securely caged, when it was only necessary to enter the trap by crawling through the top, and kill them at our leisure.

It may be asked how we made shift to cook such a thing as a turkey, other than by boiling it in a kettle, and this can be told in very few words, for it was a simple matter after once you had become accustomed to it.

A CRUDE KIND OF CHIMNEY

First you must know, however, that when our houses of logs had been built, we had nothing with which to make a chimney such as one finds in London. We had no bricks, and although, mayhap, flat rocks might have been found enough for two or three, there was no mortar in the whole land of Virginia with which to fasten them together.

Therefore it was we were forced to build a chimney of logs,

laying it up on the outside much as we had the house, but plentifully besmearing it with mud on the inside, and chinking the crevices with moss and clay.

When this had been done, a hole was cut for the smoke, directly through the side of the house. The danger of setting the building on fire was great; but we strove to guard against it so much as possible by plastering a layer of mud over the wood, and by keeping careful watch when we had a roaring fire. Oftentimes were we forced to stop in the task of cooking, take all the vessels from the coals, and throw water upon the blazing logs.

The chimney was a rude affair, of course, and perhaps if we had had women among us, they would have claimed that no cooking could be done, when all the utensils were placed directly on the burning wood, or hung above it with chains fastened to the top of the fireplace; but when lads like Nathaniel and me, who had never had any experience in cooking with proper tools, set about the task, it did not seem difficult, for we were accustomed to nothing else.

COOKING A TURKEY

And this is how we could roast a turkey: after drawing the entrails from the bird, we filled him full of chinquapin nuts, which grow profusely in this land, and are, perhaps, of some relation to the chestnut. An oaken stick, sufficiently long to reach from one side of the fireplace to the other, and trimmed with knives until it was no larger around than the ramrod of a matchlock, forms our spit, and this we thrust through the body of the bird from end to end. A pile of rocks on either side of the fireplace, at a proper distance from the burning wood, serves as rests for the ends of the wooden spit, and when thus placed the bird will be cooked in front of the fire, if whosoever is attending to the labor turns the carcass from time to time, so that each portion may receive an equal amount of heat.

I am not pretending to say that this is a skillful method of cooking; but if you had been with us in Jamestown, and were as hungry as we often were, a wild turkey filled with chinquapin nuts, and roasted in such fashion, would make a very agreeable dinner.

We were put to it for a table; but yet a sort of shelf made from a plank roughly split out of the trunk of a tree, and furnished with two legs on either end, was not as awkward as one may fancy, for we had no chairs on which to sit while eating; but squatted on the ground, and this low bench served our purpose as well as a better piece of furniture would have done.

When the captain was at home, he carved the bird with his hunting knife, and one such fowl would fill the largest trencher bowl we had among us.

Nor could we be overly nice while eating, and since we had no napkins on which to wipe our fingers, a plentiful supply of water was necessary to cleanse one's hands, for these wild turkeys are overly fat in the months of September and October, and he who holds as much of the cooked flesh in his hand as is needed for a hearty dinner, squeezes there from a considerable amount in the way of grease.

We were better off for vessels in which to put our food, than in many other respects, for we had of trencher bowls an abundance, and the London Company had outfitted us with ware of iron, or of brass, or of copper, until our poor table seemed laden with an exceeding rich store.

CANDLES OR RUSHLIGHTS

To PROVIDE LIGHTS FOR OURSELVES, now that the evenings were grown longer, was a much more difficult task than to cook without proper conveniences, for it cost considerable labor. We had our choice between the candle wood, as the pitch pine is called, or rushlights, which last are made by stripping the outer bark from common rushes, thus leaving the pith bare; then dipping these in tallow, or grease, and allowing them to harden.

In such manner did we get makeshifts for candles, neither pleasing to the eye nor affording very much in the way of light; yet they served in a certain degree to dispel the darkness when by reason of storm we were shut in the dwellings, and made the inside of the house very nearly cheerful in appearance.

To get the tallow or grease with which to make these rushlights, we saved the fat of the deer, or the bear, or even a portion of the grease from turkeys, and, having gathered sufficient for the candle making, mixed them all in one pot for melting.

The task of gathering the candle wood was more pleasing, and yet oftentimes had in it more of work, for it was the knots of the trees which gave the better light, and we might readily fasten them upon an iron skewer, or rod, which was driven into the side of the house for such purpose.

Some of our people, who were too lazy to search for knots, split the wood into small sticks, each about the size of a goose quill, and, standing three or four in a vessel filled with sand, gained as much in the way of light as might be had from one pine knot.

Of course, those who were overly particular, would find fault with the smoke from this candle wood, and complain of the tar which oozed from it; but one who lives in the wilderness must not expect to have all the luxuries that can be procured in London.

THE VISIT OF POCAHONTAS

We had a visitor from the village of Powhatan very soon after Captain Smith took command of Jamestown to such an extent that the gentlemen were forced to work and to speak without oaths, through fear of getting too much cold water inside the sleeves of their doublets.

This visitor was the same Indian girl I had seen making bread, and quite by chance our house was the first she looked into, which caused me much pride, for I believed she was attracted to it because it was more cleanly than many of the others.

We were all at home when she came, being about to partake of the noonday meal, which was neither more nor less than a big turkey weighing more than two score pounds, and roasted to a brownness

which would cause a hungry person's mouth to water.

Although she who had halted to look in at our door was only a girl, Captain Smith treated her as if she were the greatest lady in the world, himself leading her inside to his own place at the trencher-board, while she, in noways shy, began to help herself to the fattest pieces of meat, thereby besmearing herself with grease until there was enough running down her chin to have made no less than two rushlights, so Nathaniel Peacock declared.

Of course, being a savage, she could not speak in our language, but the master, who had studied diligently since coming to this world of Virginia to learn the speech of the Indians, made shift to get from her some little information, she being the daughter of Powhatan, the king concerning whom I have already set down many things.

At first Captain Smith was of the belief that she had come on some errand; but after much questioning, more by signs than words, it came out, as we understood the matter, that the girl was in Jamestown for no other purpose than to see what we white people were like.

Captain Smith was minded that she should be satisfied, so far as her curiosity was concerned, for when the dinner had come to an end, and I had given this king's daughter some dry, sweet grass on which to wipe her hands and mouth, he conducted her around the village, allowing that she look in upon the tents and houses at her pleasure.

She stayed with us until the sun was within an hour of setting, and then darted off into the forest as does a startled pheasant, stopping for a single minute when she had got among the trees, to wave her hand, as if bidding us goodbye, or in plain mischief.

CAPTAIN KENDALL'S PLOT

It is not possible my memory will serve me to tell of all that was done by us in Jamestown after we were come to our senses through the efforts of my master; but the killing of Captain Kendall is one of the many terrible happenings in Virginia, which will never be forgotten so long as I shall live.

After our people were relieved from the famine through the gifts from the Indians and the coming of wild fowl, Captain Smith set about making some plans to provide us with food during the winter, and to that end he set off in the shallop to trade with the savages, taking with him six men. He had a goodly store of beads and trinkets with which to make payment for what he might be able to buy, for these brown men are overly fond of what among English people would be little more than toys.

While he was gone, Master Wingfield and Captain Kendall were much together, for both were in a certain way under disgrace since the plot with which they charged my master had been shown to have been of their own evil imaginings. They at once set about making friends with some of the serving men, and this in itself was so strange that Nathaniel and I kept our eyes and ears open wide to discover the cause.

It was not many days before we came to know that there was a plan on foot, laid by these two men who should have been working for the good of the colony instead of to further their own base ends, to seize upon our pinnace, which lay moored to the shore, and to sail in her to England.

How that would have advantaged them I cannot even so much as guess; but certain it was that they carried on board the pinnace a great store of wild fowl, which had been cooked with much labor, and had filled two casks with water, as if believing such amount would serve to save them from thirst during the long voyage.

These wicked ones had hardly gone on board the vessel when Captain Smith came home in the shallop, which was loaded deep with Indian corn he had bought from the savages, and, seeing the pinnace being got under way, had little trouble in guessing what was afoot.

THE DEATH OF CAPTAIN KENDALL

IF EVER A MAN MOVED SWIFTLY, AND WITH PURPOSE, it was our master when he thus came to understand what Master Wingfield and Captain Kendall would do. He was on shore before those in

the pinnace could hoist the sails, and, calling upon all who remained true to the London Company to give him aid, had three of our small cannon, which were already loaded with shot, aimed at the crew of mutineers.

Five men, each with a matchlock in his hand, stood ready to fire upon those who would at the same time desert and steal from us, and Captain Smith gave the order for Captain Kendall and Master Wingfield to come on shore without delay.

For reply Captain Kendall discharged his firearm, hoping to kill my master, and then those on the bank emptied their matchlocks with such effect that Captain Kendall was killed by the first volley, causing Master Wingfield to scuttle on shore in a twinkling lest he suffer a like fate.

The whole bloody business was at an end in less than a quarter hour; but the effect of it was not so soon wiped away, for from that time each man had suspicion of his neighbor, fearing lest another attempt be made to take from us the pinnace, which we looked upon as an ark of refuge, in case the savages should come against us in such numbers that they could not be resisted.

CAPTAIN SMITH'S EXPEDITION AND RETURN

UNTIL WINTER WAS COME WE HAD FOOD IN PLENTY, for one could hardly send a charge of shot toward the river without bringing down swans, ducks, or cranes, while from the savages we got sufficient for our daily wants, meal made from the corn, pumpkins, peas, and beans.

But this did not cause Captain Smith to give over trying to buy from the Indians a store of corn for the winter, and shortly after

Captain Kendall's death, he set off with nine white men and two Indian guides in a barge, counting to go as far as the head of the Chickahominy River.

This time twenty-two long, dreary days went by without his return, and we mourned him as dead, believing the savages had murdered him.

The discontented ones were in high glee because of thinking the man who had forced them to do that which they should, had gone out from their world forever, and we two lads were plunged in deepest grief, for in all the great land of Virginia, Captain Smith was our only true friend.

Then arrived that day when he suddenly appeared before us, having come to no harm, and as Master Hunt lifted up his hands in a prayer of thanksgiving because the man who was so sadly needed in Jamestown had returned, I fell on my knees, understanding for the first time in my life how good God could be to us in that wilderness.

I would that I might describe the scene in our house that night, when Master Hunt was come to hear what all knew would be a story of wildest adventure, for it went without saying that my master never would have remained so long absent from Jamestown had it been within his power to return sooner.

AN EXCITING ADVENTURE

WE WAITED TO HEAR THE TALE until he had refreshed himself after the long journey, and then what Captain Smith told us was like unto this, as I remember it:

After leaving the village, he had sailed up the river until there was no longer water enough to float the barge, when, with two white men and the two Indians, he embarked in a canoe, continuing the voyage for a distance of twelve miles or more. There, in the wilderness, they made ready to spend the night, and with one of the savage guides my master went on shore on an island to shoot some wild fowls for supper. He had traveled a short distance from the boat, when he heard cries of the savages in the distance, and, looking back, saw that one of the men had been taken prisoner, while the other was fighting for his life.

At almost the very minute when he saw this terrible thing, he was suddenly beset by more than two hundred yelling, dancing savages,

who were sweeping down upon him as if believing he was in their power beyond any chance. The Indian guide, who appeared to be terribly frightened, although it might have been that he was in the plot to murder my master, would have run away; but that Captain Smith held him fast while he fired one of his pistols to keep the enemy in check.

Understanding that he must do battle for his life, my master first took the precaution to bind the Indian guide to his left arm, by means of his belt, in such fashion that the fellow would serve as a shield against the shower of arrows the savages were sending through the air.

Protected in this manner, Captain Smith fought bravely, as he always does, and had succeeded in killing two of the Indians with his matchlock, when suddenly he sank knee deep into a mire. It seems that he had been retreating toward the canoe, hoping to get on board her where would be some chance for shelter, and was so engaged with the savages in front of him as to give little heed to his steps.

Once he was held prisoner by the mud, the enemy quickly surrounded him, and he could do no better than surrender. Instead of treating him cruelly, as might have been expected, these brown men carried him from village to village, as if exhibiting some strange animal.

TAKEN BEFORE POWHATAN

WHEN HE WAS FIRST MADE CAPTIVE, the Indians found his compass, and were stricken with wonder, because, however the instrument might be turned, the needle always pointed in the same direction. The glass which protected the needle caused even more amazement, and, believing him to be a magician, they took him to Powhatan.

After many days of traveling, the savages were come with their prisoner to Powhatan's village, where Captain Smith was held close prisoner in one of the huts, being fairly well treated and fed in abundance, until the king, who had been out with a hunting party, came home.

Twice while he was thus captive did Captain Smith see the girl Pocahontas, who had visited him in Jamestown; but she gave no especial heed to him, save as a child who was minded to be amused, until on the day when some of the savages gave him to understand that he was to be killed for having come into this land of theirs, and also for having shot to death some of their tribe.

When he was led out of Powhatan's tent of skins, with his feet and hands bound, he had no hope of being able to save his own life, for there was no longer any chance for him to struggle against those who had him in their power.

POCAHONTAS BEGS FOR SMITH'S LIFE

HE WAS FORCED DOWN ON THE EARTH, with his head upon a great rock, while two half naked savages came forward with heavy stones bound to wooden handles, with which to beat out his

brains, and these weapons were already raised to strike, when the girl Pocahontas ran forward, throwing herself upon my master, as she asked that Powhatan give him to her.

Now, as we afterward came to know, it is the custom among savages, that when one of their women begs for the life of a prisoner, to grant the prayer, and so it was done in this case, else we had never seen my master again.

It is also the custom, when a prisoner has thus been given to one who begged for his life, that the captive shall always be held as slave by her; but Pocahontas desired only to let him go back to Jamestown. Then it was she told her father how she had been treated when visiting us, and Powhatan, after keeping Captain Smith prisoner until he could tell of what he had seen in other countries of the world, set him free.

THE EFFECT OF CAPTAIN SMITH'S RETURN

It was well for us of Jamestown that my master returned just when he did, for already had our gentlemen, believing him dead, refused longer to work, and even neglected the hunting, when game of all kinds was so plentiful. They had spent the time roaming around searching for gold, until we were once more in need of food.

The sickness had come among us again, and of all our company, which numbered an hundred when Captain Newport sailed for England, only thirty-eight remained alive.

Within four and twenty hours after Captain Smith came back, matters had so far mended that every man who could move about at will, was working for the common good, although from that time, until Captain Newport came again, we had much of suffering.

With the coming of winter Nathaniel and I were put to it to do our work in anything like a seemly manner. What with the making of candles, or of rushlights; tanning deer hides in such fashion as Captain Smith had taught us; mending his doublets of leather, as well as our own; keeping the house and  ground around it fairly clean, in addition to cooking meals which might tempt the appetite of our master, we were busy from sunrise to sunset.

Nor were we without our reward. On rare occasions Captain Smith would commend us for attending to our duties in better fashion than he had fancied lads would ever be able to do, and very often did Master Hunt whisper words of praise in our ears, saying again and again that he would there were in his house two boys like us.

This you may be sure was more of payment than we had a reasonable right to expect, for certain it is that even at our best the work was but fairly done, as it ever must be when there are houseboys instead of housewives at home.

Master Hunt had a serving man, William Rods, and he was not one well fitted to do a woman's work, for in addition to being clumsy, even at the expense of breaking now and then a wooden trencher bowl, he had no thought that cleanliness was, as the preacher often told us, next to godliness.

It was he, and such as he, that caused Captain Smith and those others of the Council who were minded to work for the common good, very much of trouble.

The rule, as laid down by my master, was that those living in a dwelling should keep cleanly the land roundabout the outside for a space of five yards, and yet again and again have I seen William Rods throw the refuse from the table just outside the door, meaning to take it away at a future time, and always forgetting so to do until reminded by some one in authority.

However, it is not for me to speak of such trifling things as these, although had you heard Captain Smith and Master Hunt in conversation, you would not have set them down as being of little importance. Those two claimed that only by strict regard to cleanliness, both of person and house, would it be possible for us, when another summer came, to ward off that sickness which had already carried away so many of our company.

After Captain Smith had brought matters to rights in the village, setting this company of men to building more houses, and that company to hewing down trees for firewood, which would be needed when the winter had come, Master Hunt made mention of a matter which I knew must have been very near his heart many a day.

A NEW CHURCH

During all the time we had been on shore, the only church in Jamestown was the shelter beneath that square of canvas which he himself had put up. When it stormed, he had called such of the people as were inclined to worship into one or another of the houses; but now he asked that a log building be put together, while it was yet so warm that the men could work out of doors without suffering, and to this, much to my pleasure, for I had an exceedingly friendly feeling toward Master Hunt, Captain Smith agreed.

Therefore it was that when the storms of October came, Master Hunt had a place in which to receive those whom he would lead to a better life, and I believe that all our people, the men who were careless regarding the future life, and those who followed the preacher's teachings, felt the better in mind because there was at last in our village a place which would be used for no other purpose than that of leading us into, and helping us to remain in, the straight path.

CAPTAIN NEWPORT'S RETURN

It was at the beginning of the new year, two days after my master was set free by the savages, that Captain Newport came back to us, this time in the ship *John and Francis*, and with him were fifty men who had been sent to join our colony.

Fortunately for us there were but few gentlemen among them, therefore did the work of building the village go on much more rapidly, because there were laborers in plenty.

A larger building, which was called the fort, and would indeed have been a safe place for refuge had the savages made an attack, was but just completed at the beginning of the third month, meaning March.

There Captain Smith had stored the supply of provisions and seed brought in the *John and Francis*, and we were already saying to ourselves that by the close of the summer we should reap a bountiful harvest.

All these plans and hopes went for naught, however, for on a certain night, and no man can say how it happened, save him who was the careless one, fire fastened upon the inside of the fort, having so much headway when it was discovered, that our people could do little toward checking it.

The flames burst out through the roof, which was thatched with dried grass, as were all the houses in the town, and leaped from one building to another until it seemed as if the entire village would be destroyed.

It is true that even the palisade, which was near to forty feet distant from the fort, was seized upon by the flames, and a goodly portion of that which had cost us so much labor was entirely destroyed.

Out of all our houses only four remained standing when the flames had died away. The seed which we had counted on for reaping a harvest, the store of provisions, and a large amount of clothing and other necessaries, were thus consumed.

Good Master Hunt lost all his books, in fact, everything he owned save the clothes upon his back, and yet never once did I, who was with him very much, for he came to live at our house while the village was being rebuilt, hear him utter one word of complaint, or of sorrow.

GOLD-SEEKERS

It was while all the people, gentlemen as well as laborers, were doing their best to repair the loss, and to put Jamestown into such shape that we might be able to withstand an attack from the savages, if so be they made one, that even a worse misfortune than the fire came upon us.

Some of those whom Captain Newport had lately brought to Virginia, while roaming along the shores of the river in order to learn what this new land was like, came upon a spot where the waters had washed the earth away for a distance of five or six feet, leaving exposed to view a vast amount of sand, so yellow and so heavy that straightway the foolish ones believed they were come upon that gold which our people had been seeking almost from the very day we first landed.

From this moment there was no talk of anything save the wealth which would come to us and the London Company.

Even Captain Newport was persuaded that this sand was gold, and straightway nearly every person in the village was hard at work digging and carrying it in baskets on board the *John and Francis* as carefully as if each grain counted for a guinea.

Of all the people of Jamestown, Captain Smith and Master Hunt were the only ones who refused to believe the golden dream. They held themselves aloof from this mad race to gather up the yellow

sand, and strove earnestly to persuade the others that it would be a simple matter to prove by fire whether this supposed treasure were metal.

In the center of the village, where all might see him, Master Hunt set a pannikin, in which was a pint or more of the sand, over a roaring fire which he kept burning not less than two hours.

When he was done, the sand remained the same as before, which, so he and my master claimed, was good proof that our people of Jamestown were, in truth, making fools of themselves, as they had many a time before since we came into this land of Virginia.

A WORTHLESS CARGO

W<small>HEN WE SHOULD HAVE BEEN STRIVING</small> to build up the town once more, we spent all our time loading the ship with this worthless cargo, and indeed I felt the better in my mind when finally Captain Newport set sail, the *John and Francis* loaded deeply with sand, because of believing that we were come to an end of hearing about treasure which lay at hand ready for whosoever would carry it away.

In this, however, I was disappointed. Although there was no longer any reason for our people to labor at what was called the gold mine, since there was no ship at hand in which to put the sand, they still talked, hour by hour, of the day when all the men in Virginia would go back to England richer than kings.

Because of such thoughts was it well nigh impossible to force them to labor once more. Yet Captain Smith and Master Hunt did all they could, even going so far as to threaten bodily harm if the people did not rebuild the storehouse, plant such seed as had been saved from the flames, and replace those portions of the palisade which had been burned.

It was while our people were thus working half heartedly, that Captain Nelson arrived in the ship *Phoenix*, having been so long delayed on the voyage, because of tempests and contrary winds, that his passengers and crew had eaten nearly all the stores which the London Company sent over for our benefit, and bringing seventy more mouths to be fed.

Save that she brought to us skilled workmen, the coming of the *Phoenix* did not advantage us greatly, while there were added to our number, seventy men, and of oatmeal, pickled beef and pork, as much as would serve for, perhaps, three or four weeks.

Through her, however, as Master Hunt said in my hearing, came some little good, for on seeing the yellow sand, Captain Nelson declared without a question that it was worthless, and, being accustomed to working in metal, speedily proved to our people who were yet suffering with the gold fever, that there was nothing whatsoever of value in it.

THE CONDITION OF THE COLONY

That he might have something to carry back to England, and not being minded to take on board a load of sand, Captain Nelson asked that the *Phoenix* be laden with cedar logs and such clapboards as our people had made. Therefore was it that we sent to England the first cargo of value since having come to Virginia.

Among those who had come over in the *Phoenix* were workmen who understood the making of turpentine, tar and soap ashes. There was also a pipe maker, a gunsmith, and a number of other skilled workmen, so that had the Council advanced the interest of the colony one half as much as my master was doing, all would have gone well with us in Jamestown.

As it was, however, the President of the Council, so Master Hunt has declared many times, and of a verity he would not bear false witness, often countenanced the men in rebellion against my master's orders, until, but for the preacher's example, we might never have put into the earth our first seed.

Because of lack of food, and it seems strange to say so when there were of oysters near at hand more than a thousand men could have eaten, and fish in the rivers without number, Captain Smith set off once more in the pinnace to trade with the Indians, as well as to explore further the bay and the river.

Master Hunt lived in our house, while he was gone, therefore Nathaniel and I were not idle, and though we had each had a dozen pair of hands, we could have kept them properly employed, what with making a garden for our own use, tending the plants, and keeping house.

TOBACCO

Just here I am minded to set down that which the girl Pocahontas told us concerning the raising of tobacco, and it is well she spent the time needed to instruct us, for since then I have seen the people in this new world of Virginia getting more money from the tobacco plant, than they could have gained even though Captain

Newport's yellow sand had been veritable gold.

You must know that the seed of tobacco is even smaller than grains of powder, and the Indians usually plant it in April. Within a month it springs up, each tiny plant having two or four leaves, and one month later it is transplanted in little hillocks, set about the same distance apart as are our hills of Indian corn.

Two or three times during the season the plants have to be hoed and weeded, while the sickly leaves, which peep out from the body of the stock, must be plucked off.

If the plant grows too fast, which is to say, if it is like to get its full size before harvest time, the tops are cut to make it more backward.

About the middle of September it is reaped, stripped of its leaves, and tied in small bunches; these are hung under a shelter so that the dew may not come to them, until they are cured the same as hay.

Having thus been dried, and there must be no suspicion of moisture about, else they will mold, the whole is packed into hogsheads.

I have lived to see the days go by since the girl Pocahontas showed Nathaniel and me how to cultivate the weed, until the greatest wealth which Virginia can produce comes from this same tobacco, which, Master Hunt says, not only induces filthiness in those who use it, but works grievous injury to the body.

CAPTAIN NEWPORT'S RETURN

When Captain Newport came back to Virginia, at about the time we were gathering our scanty harvest, his dreams of sudden wealth, through the digging of gold in Virginia, had burst as does a bubble when one pricks it.

He had not been more than four and twenty hours in England before learning that his ship was laden only with valueless sand, and, mayhap, if the London Company had not demanded that he return to Virginia at once, with certain orders concerning us at Jamestown, he might have been too much ashamed to show his face among us again.

My master had come in long since from trading with the Indians, having had fairly good success at times, and again failing utterly to gather food. The king Powhatan was grown so lofty in his bearing, because of the honor some of our foolish people had shown him, that it was well nigh impossible to pay the price he asked, even in trinkets, for so small an amount as a single peck of corn.

However, that which Powhatan did or did not do, concerned me very little when Captain Newport had arrived, for he brought with him such tidings as made my heart rejoice, and caused Master Hunt to say that now indeed would our village of Jamestown grow as it should have grown had our leaders shown themselves of half as much spirit as had my master.

But for the greater things which followed Captain Newport's arrival in September of the year 1608, I would have set it down as of the utmost importance to us in Jamestown, that he brought with him the first two women, other than the girl Pocahontas, who had ever come into our town.

These were Mistress Forest, and her maid, Anne Burras, and if the king himself had so far done us the honor as to come, his arrival would have caused no greater excitement.

GAZING AT THE WOMEN

EVERY MAN AND BOY IN THE SETTLEMENT pressed forward eager even to touch the garments of these two women as they came ashore in the ship's small boat, and I dare venture to say that we stared at them, Nathaniel and I among the number, even as the savages stared at us when first we landed.

It would have been more to my satisfaction had there been two maids, instead of only one and her mistress, for it was more than likely servants could tell Nathaniel and me many things about our care of the house, which a great lady would not well know. Therefore, as I viewed the matter, we could well spare fine women, so that we had maids who would understand of what we as houseboys stood mostly in need.

However, it was not with these women, who were only two among seventy, that had come with Captain Newport on this his

third voyage, that I was most deeply concerned, and how I learned that which pleased me so greatly shall be set down exactly as it happened.

MASTER HUNT BRINGS GREAT NEWS

I HAD BEEN DOWN AT THE LANDING PLACE, feasting my eyes upon the ship which had so lately come from the country I might never see again, and was trying to cheer myself by working around the house in the hope of pleasing Captain Smith, when Master Hunt came in with a look upon his face such as I had not seen since the sickness first came among us, and, without thinking to be rude, I asked him if it was the arrival of the women which pleased him so greatly.

"It is nothing of such fanciful nature, Richard Mutton," the good man replied with a smile, "though I must confess that it is pleasing to see women with white faces, when our eyes have beheld none save bearded men for so long a time. What think you has been done in the Council this day, since Captain Newport had speech with President Ratcliffe?"

Verily I could not so much as guess what might have happened, for those worshipful gentlemen were prone at times to behave more like foolish children, than men upon whom the fate of a new country depended, and I said to Master Hunt much of the same purport.

"They have elected your master, Captain John Smith, President of the Council, Richard Mutton, and now for the first time will matters in Jamestown progress as they should."

"My master President of the Council at last!" I cried, and the good preacher added:

"So it is, lad, as I know full well, having just come from there."

"But how did they chance suddenly to gather their wits?" I cried with a laugh, in which Master Hunt joined.

"It was done after Captain Newport had speech with Master Ratcliffe, and while I know nothing for a certainty, there is in my mind a strong belief that he brought word from the London Company for such an election to be made. At all events, it is done, and now we shall see Jamestown increase in size, even as she would have done from the first month we landed here had Captain John Smith been at the head of affairs."

The good preacher was so delighted with this change in the government that he unfolded all his budget of news, forgetting for the time being, most like, that he was not speaking to his equal, and thus it was I learned what were Captain Newport's instructions from the London Company.

CAPTAIN NEWPORT'S INSTRUCTIONS

HE WAS ORDERED, IF YOU PLEASE, not to return to England without bringing back a lump of gold, exploring the passageway to the South Sea, or finding some of Sir Walter Raleigh's lost colony, of which I will tell you later.

But whether he did the one or the other, he had been commanded to crown as a king, Powhatan, and had brought with him mock jewels and red robes for such a purpose.

To find a lump of gold, after he had brought to England a shipload of yellow sand!

To crown Powhatan king, when, to our sorrow, he was already showing himself far more of a king than was pleasing or well for our town of James!

Forgetting I was but a lad, and had no right to put blame on the shoulders of my leaders and betters, or even to address Master Hunt as if I were a man grown, I cried out against the foolishness of those people in London for whom we were striving to build up a city, saying very much that had better been left unsaid, until the good preacher cried with a laugh:

"We can forgive them almost anything, Dicky Mutton, since they have made our Captain Smith the head of the government in this land of Virginia."

And now I will tell you, as Master Hunt told me, the story of this lost colony of Roanoke, which the London Company had commanded Captain Newport to find.

You must know that English people had lived in this land of Virginia before we came here in 1606, and while it does not concern us of Jamestown, except as we are interested in knowing the fate of our countrymen, it should be set down, lest we so far forget as to say that those of us who have built this village are the first settlers in the land.

THE STORY OF ROANOKE

Twenty-one years before we sailed from London, Sir Walter Raleigh sent out a fleet of seven ships, carrying one hundred and seven persons, to Virginia, and Master Ralph Lane was named as the governor. They landed on Roanoke Island; but because the Indians threatened them, and because just at that time when they were most frightened, Sir Francis Drake came by with his fleet, they all went home, not daring to stay any longer.

Two years after that, which is to say nineteen years before we of Jamestown came here, Sir Walter Raleigh sent over one hundred and sixteen people, among whom were men, women and children, and they also began to build a town on Roanoke Island.

John White was their governor, and very shortly after they came to Roanoke, his daughter, Mistress Ananias Dare, had a little baby girl, the first white child to be born in the new world, so they named her Virginia.

Now these people, like ourselves, were soon sorely in need of food, and they coaxed Governor John White to go back to England, to get what would be needed until they could gather a harvest.

At the time he arrived at London, England was at war with the Spanish people, and it was two years before he found a chance to get back. When he finally arrived at Roanoke Island, there were no signs of any of his people to be found, except that on the tree was cut the word "Croatan," which is the name of an Indian village on the island nearby.

That was the last ever heard of all those hundred and sixteen people. Five different times Sir Walter Raleigh sent out men for the missing ones; but no traces could be found, not even at Croatan, and no one knows whether they were killed by the Indians, or wandered off into the wilderness where they were lost forever.

You can see by the story, that the London Company had set for Captain Newport a very great task when they commanded him to do what so many people had failed in before him.

And now out of that story of the lost colony, as Master Hunt told Nathaniel and me, grows another which also concerns us in this new land of Virginia.

You will remember I have said that Master Ralph Lane was the governor of the first company of people who went to Roanoke Island, and, afterward, getting discouraged, returned to England. Now this Master Lane, and the other men who were with him, learned from the Indians to smoke the weed called tobacco, and carried quite a large amount of it home with them.

Not only Sir Walter Raleigh, who knew Master Lane very well, but many other people in England also learned to smoke, and therefore it was that when we of Jamestown began to raise tobacco, it found a more ready sale in London than any other thing we could send over. Once this was known, our people gave the greater portion of their time to cultivating the Indian weed.

THE CROWNING OF POWHATAN

VERY NEARLY THE FIRST THING WHICH MY MASTER DID after having been made President of the Council, was to obey the orders of the

London Company, by going with Captain Newport to Powhatan's village in order to crown him like a king.

This was not at all to the pleasure of the savage, who failed of understanding what my master and Captain Newport meant, when they wanted him to kneel down so they might put the crown upon his head. If all the stories which I have heard regarding the matter are true, they must have had quite a scrimmage before succeeding in getting him into what they believed was a proper position to receive the gifts of the London Company.

Our people, so Master Hunt told me, were obliged to take him by the shoulders and force him to his knees, after which they clapped the crown on his head, and threw the red robe around his shoulders in a mighty hurry lest he show fight and overcome them.

It was some time before Captain Smith could make him understand that it was a great honor which was being done him, but when he did get it through his head, he took off his old moccasins and brought from the hut his raccoon skin coat, with orders that my master and Captain Newport send them all to King James in London, as a present from the great Powhatan of Virginia.

After this had been done, Captain Newport sailed up the James River in search of the passage to the South Sea, and my master set about putting Jamestown into proper order.

PREPARING FOR THE FUTURE

ONCE MORE CAPTAIN SMITH MADE THE RULE that those who would not work should not eat, and this time, with all the Council at his back, together with such men as Captain Newport had just brought

with him, you can well fancy his orders were obeyed.

In addition to the stocks which had been built, he had a pillory set up, and those gentlemen who were not inclined to labor with their hands as well as they might, were forced to stand in it to their discomfort.

The next thing which he did was to have a large, deep well dug, so that we might have sweet water from it for drinking purposes, rather than be forced to use that from the river, for it was to his mind that through this muddy water did the sickness come to us.

When the winter was well begun, and Captain Newport ceased to search for the South Sea passage, because of having come to the falls of the James River, Captain Smith forced our people to build twenty stout houses such as would serve to withstand an attack from the savages, and again was the palisade stretched from one to the other, until the village stood in the form of a square.

After the cold season had passed, some of the people were set about shingling the church, and others were ordered to make clapboards that we might have a cargo when Captain Newport returned. It was the duty of some few to keep the streets and lanes of the village clear of filth, lest we invite the sickness again, and the remainder of the company were employed in planting Indian corn, forty acres of which were seeded down.

STEALING THE COMPANY'S GOODS

IF I HAVE MADE IT APPEAR THAT DURING ALL THIS TIME we lived in the most friendly manner with the savages, then have I blundered in the setting down of that which happened.

Although it shames one to write such things concerning those who called themselves Englishmen, yet it must be said that the savages were no longer in any degree friendly, and all because of what our own people had done.

From the time when Captain Smith had declared that he who would not work should not eat, some of our fine gentlemen who were willing to believe that labor was the greatest crime which could be committed, began stealing from the common store iron and copper goods of every kind which might be come at, in order to trade with the savages for food they themselves were too lazy to get otherwise.

They even went so far, some of those who thought it more the part of a man to wear silks than build himself a house, as to steal

matchlocks, pistols, and weapons of any kind, standing ready to teach the savages how to use these things, if thereby they were given so much additional in the way of food.

As our numbers increased, by reason of the companies which were brought over by Captain Newport and Captain

Nelson, so did the thievery become the more serious until on one day I heard Master Hunt tell my master, that of forty axes which had been brought ashore from the *Phoenix* and left outside the storehouse during the night, but eight were remaining when morning came.

WHAT THE THIEVING LED TO

Now there was more of mischief to this than the crime of stealing, or of indolence. The savages came to understand they could drive hard bargains, and so increased the price of their corn that Captain Smith set it down in his report to the London Company, that the same amount of copper, or of beads, which had, one year before, paid for five bushels of wheat, would, within a week after Captain Newport came in search of the lost colony, pay for no more than one peck.

Nor was this the entire sum of the wrong done by our gentlemen who stole rather than worked with their hands. The savages, grown bold now that they had firearms and knew how to use them, no longer had the same fear of white people as when Captain Smith, single handed, was able to hold two hundred in check, and strove to kill us of Jamestown whenever they found opportunity.

On four different times did they plot to murder my master, believing that when he had been done to death, it would be more easy for them to kill off all in our town; but on each occasion, so keen was his watchfulness, he outwitted them all.

The putting of a crown on Powhatan's head, and bowing before him as if he had been a real king, also did much mischief. It caused that brown savage to believe we feared him, which was much the same as inviting him to be less of a friend, until on a certain day he boldly declared that one basket of his corn was worth more than all our copper and beads, because he could eat his corn, while our trinkets gave a hungry man no satisfaction.

And thus, by the wicked and unwise acts of our own people, did we prepare the way for another time of famine and sickness.

FEAR OF FAMINE IN A LAND OF PLENTY

However, I must set this much down as counting in our favor: when we landed in this country we had three pigs, and a cock and six hens, all of which we turned loose in the wilderness to shift for themselves, giving shelter to such as came back to us when winter was near at hand.

Within two years we had of pigs more than sixty, in addition to many which were yet running wild in the forest. Of hens and cocks we had upward of five hundred, the greater number being kept in pens to the end that we might profit by their eggs.

I have heard Master Hunt declare more than once, that had we followed Captain Smith's advice, giving all our labor to the raising of crops, our storehouse would have been too small for the food on

hand, and we might have held ourselves free from the whims of the savages, having corn to sell, rather than spending near to half our time trying to buy.

As Master Hunt said again and again when talking over the situation with Captain Smith, it seemed strange even to us who were there, that we could be looking forward to a famine, when in the sea and on the land was food in abundance to feed half the people in all this wide world.

To show how readily one might get himself a dinner, if so be his taste were not too nice, I have seen Captain Smith, when told what we had in the larder for the next meal, go to the river with only his naked sword, and there spear fish enough with the weapon to provide us with as much as could be eaten in a full day. But yet some of our gentlemen claimed that it was not good for their blood to eat this food of the sea; others declared that oysters, when partaken of regularly, were as poisonous as the sweet potatoes which we bought of the Indians.

Thus it was that day by day did we who were in the land of plenty, overrun with that which would serve as food, fear that another time of famine was nigh.

THE UNHEALTHFUL LOCATION

I HAVE OFTEN SPOKEN OF THE UNWILLINGNESS of some of our people to labor; but Captain Smith, who is not overly eager to find excuses for those who are indolent, has said that there was much reason why many of our men hugged their cabins, counting it a most arduous task to go even so far up the river as were the oyster-beds.

He believes, and Master Hunt is of the same opinion, that this town of ours has been built on that portion of the shore where the people are most liable to sickness. The land is low-lying, almost on a level with the river; the country roundabout is made up of swamps and bogs, and the air which comes to us at night is filled with a fever, which causes those upon whom it fastens, first to shake as if they were beset with bitterest cold, and then again to burn as if likely to be reduced to ashes. Some call it the ague, and others, the shakes; but whatsoever it may be, there is nothing more distressing, or better calculated to hinder a man from taking so much of exercise as is necessary for his well being.

GATHERING OYSTERS

THAT NATHANIEL AND I MAY GATHER OYSTERS without too great labor of walking and carrying heavy burdens, Captain Smith has bought from the savages a small boat made of the bark of birch trees, stretched over a framework of splints, and sewn together with the entrails of deer. On the seams, and wherever the water might find entrance, it is well gummed with pitch taken from the pine tree, and withal the lightest craft that can well be made.

Either Nathaniel or I can take this vessel, which the savages call a canoe, on our shoulders, carrying it without difficulty, and when the two of us are inside, resting upon our knees, for we may not sit in it as in a ship's boat, we can send it along with paddles at a rate so rapid as to cause one to think it moved by magic.

With this canoe Nathaniel and I may go to the oyster- beds, and in half an hour put on board as large a cargo of shellfish as she will carry, in addition to our own weight, coming back in a short time with as much food as would serve a dozen men for two days.

If these oysters could be kept fresh for any length of time, then would we have a most valuable store near at hand; but, like other fish, a few hours in the sun serves to spoil them.

PREPARING STURGEON FOR FOOD

Of the fish called the sturgeon, we have more than can be consumed by all our company; but one cannot endure the flavor day after day, and therefore is it that we use it for food only when we cannot get any other.

Master Hunt has shown Nathaniel and me how we may prepare it in such a manner as to change the flavor. It must first be dried in the sun until so hard that it can be pounded to the fineness of meal. This is then mixed with caviare, by which I mean the eggs, or roe, of the sturgeon, with sorrel leaves, and with other wholesome herbs. The whole is made into small balls, or cakes, which are fried over the fire with a plentiful amount of fat.

Such a dish serves us for either bread or meat, or for both on a pinch, therefore if we lads are careful not to waste our time, Captain Smith may never come without finding in the larder something that can be eaten.

TURPENTINE AND TAR

To us in Jamestown the making of anything which we may send back to England for sale, is of such great importance that we are more curious regarding the manner in which the work is done,

than would be others who are less eager to see piled up that which will bring money to the people.

Therefore it was that Nathaniel and I watched eagerly the making of turpentine, and found it not unlike the method by which the Indians gain sugar from maple trees. A strip of bark is taken from the pine, perhaps eight or ten inches long, and at the lower end of the wound thus made, a deep notch is cut in the wood. Into this the sap flows, and is scraped out as fast as the cavity is filled. It is a labor in which all may join, and so plentiful are the pine trees that if our people of Jamestown set about making turpentine only, they might load four or five ships in a year.

From the making of tar much money can be earned, and it is a simple process such as I believe I myself might compass, were it not that I have sufficient of other work to occupy all my time.

The pine tree is cut into short pieces, even the roots being used, for, if I mistake not, more tar may be had from the roots than from the

trunks of the tree. Our people here dig a hollow, much like unto the shape of a funnel, on the side of a hill, or bank, fill it in with the wood and the roots, and cover the whole closely with turf.

An iron pot is placed at the bottom of this hollow in the earth, and a fire is built at the top of the pile. While the fuel smolders, the tar stews out of the wood, falling into the iron pot, and from there is put into whatsoever vessels may be most convenient in which to carry it over seas.

THE MAKING OF CLAPBOARDS

THERE IS FAR GREATER LABOR REQUIRED IN THE MAKING of clapboards, and it is of a wearisome kind; but Captain Newport declares that clapboards made of our Virginia cedar are far better in quality than any to be found in England. Therefore it is Captain Smith keeps as many men as he may, employed in this work, which is more tiring than difficult.

The trunks of the trees are cut into lengths of four feet, and trimmed both as to branches and bark. An iron tool called a frow, which is not unlike a butcher's cleaver, is then used to split the log into thin strips, one edge of which is four or five times thicker than the other.

You will understand better the method by picturing to yourself the end of a round log which has been stood upright for convenience of the workmen. Now, if you place a frow in such a position that it will split the thicknesses of an inch or less from the outer side, you will find that the point of the instrument, which is at the heart of the tree, must come in such manner as to make the splint very thin on the inner edge. The frow is driven through the wood by a wooden mallet, to the end that the sides of the clapboard may be fairly smooth.

Master Hunt has told me that if we were to put on board a ship the size of the *John and Francis*, as many clapboards as she could swim under, the value of the cargo would be no less than five hundred pounds, and they would have a ready sale in London, or in other English ports.

PROVIDING FOR THE CHILDREN

AND NOW BEFORE I AM COME TO THE MOST TERRIBLE time in the history of our town of James, let me set down that which the London Company has decreed, for it is of great importance to all those who, like Nathaniel and me, came over into this land of Virginia before they were men and women grown.

Master Hunt has written the facts out fairly, to the end that I may understand them well, he having had the information from Captain Newport, for it was the last decree made by the London Company before the *John and Francis* sailed.

I must say, however, that the reason why this decree, or order, whichever it may be called, has been made, was to the end that men and women, who had large families of children, might be induced to join us here in Jamestown, as if we had not already mouths enough to feed.

The Council of the Company has decided to allow the use of twenty-five acres of land for each and every child that comes into Virginia, and all who are now here, or may come to live at the expense of the Company, are to be educated in some good trade or profession, in order that they may be able to support themselves when they have come to the age of four and twenty years, or have served the time of their apprenticeship, which is to be no less than seven years.

It is further decreed that all of those children when they become of age or marry, whichever shall happen first, are to have freely given and made over to them fifty acres of land apiece, which same shall be in Virginia within the limits of the English plantation. But, these children must be placed as apprentices under honest and good masters within the grant made to the London Company, and shall serve for seven years, or until they come to the age of twenty-four, during which time their masters must bring them up in some trade or business.

DREAMS OF THE FUTURE

ON HEARING THIS, THE QUESTION CAME INTO MY MIND as to whether Nathaniel and I could be called apprentices, inasmuch as we were only houseboys, according to the name Captain Smith gave us.

Master Hunt declared that being apprentices to care for the family, was of as much service as if we were learned in the trade of making tar, clapboards, or of building ships, and he assured me that if peradventure he was living when we had been in this land of Virginia seven years, it should be his duty to see to it that we were given our fifty acres of land apiece.

Thus understanding that we might ourselves in turn one day

become planters, Nathaniel and I had much to say, one with the other, concerning what should be done in the future. We decided that when the time came for us to have the land set off to our own use, we would strive that the two lots of fifty acres each be in one piece. Then would we set about raising tobacco, as the Indian girl Pocahontas taught us, and who can say that we might not come to be of some consequence, even as are Captain Smith and Master Hunt, in this new world.

A PLAGUE OF RATS

AND NOW AM I COME TO THE SPRING OF 1609, when befell us that disaster which marked the beginning of the time of suffering, of trouble, and of danger which was so near to wiping out the settlement of Jamestown that the people had already started on their way to England.

The day had come when we should put into the ground our Indian corn that a harvest might follow. The supply, which was to be used as seed, had been stored in casks and piled up in the big house wherein were kept our goods.

When those who had been chosen to do the planting went for the seed, it was found to have been destroyed by rats, and not only the corn, but many other things which were in the storehouse, had been eaten by the same animals.

Master Hunt maintained, and Captain Smith was of the same opinion, that when the *Phoenix* was unloaded, the rats came ashore from her, finding lodging in that building which represented the vital spot of our town.

Howsoever the pests came there, certain it was we should reap no harvest that year, unless the savages became more friendly than they had lately shown themselves, and as to this we speedily learned.

TREACHERY DURING CAPTAIN SMITH'S ABSENCE

WHEN CAPTAIN SMITH SET OFF IN THE PINNACE in order to buy what might serve us as seed, he found himself threatened by all the brown  men living near about the shores of the bay, as if they had suddenly made up a plot to kill us, and never one of them would speak him fairly.

It was while my master was away that two Dutchmen, who came over in the *Phoenix* and had gone with Captain Smith in the pinnace, returned to Jamestown, saying to Captain Winne, who was in command at the fort, that Captain Smith had use for more weapons because of going into the country in the hope of finding Indians who would supply him with corn.

Not doubting their story, the captain supplied them with what they demanded, and, as was afterward learned, before leaving town that night they stole many swords, pike heads, shot and powder, all of which these Dutch thieves carried to Powhatan.

If these two had been the only white men who did us wrong, then might our plight not have become so desperate; but many there were, upwards of sixteen so Master Hunt declared, who from day to day carried away secretly such weapons and tools, or powder and shot, as they could come upon, thereby trusting to the word of the savages that they might live with them in their villages always, without doing any manner of work.

Others sold kettles, hoes, or even swords and guns, that they might buy fruit, or corn, or meat from the Indians without doing so much of labor as was necessary in order to gather these things for themselves.

CAPTAIN SMITH'S SPEECH

JAMESTOWN WAS A SCENE OF TURMOIL AND CONFUSION when Captain Smith came back from his journey having on board only two baskets of corn for seed. After understanding what had been done by the idle ones during his absence, he called all the people together and said unto them, speaking earnestly, as if pleading for his very life:

"Never did I believe white men who were come together in a new world, and should stand shoulder to shoulder against all the enemies that surround them, could be so reckless and malicious. It is vain to hope for more help from Powhatan, and the time has come when I will no longer bear with you in your idleness; but punish severely if you do not set about the work which must be done, without further plotting. You cannot deny but that I have risked my life many a time in order to save yours, when, if you had been allowed to go your own way, all would have starved. Now I swear solemnly that you shall not only gather for yourselves the fruits which the earth doth yield, but for those who are sick. Every one that gathers not each day as much as I do, shall on the next day be set beyond the river, forever banished from the fort, to live or starve as God wills."

This caused the lazy ones to bestir themselves for the time, and perhaps all might have gone well with us had not the London Company sent out nine more vessels, in which were five hundred persons, to join us people in Jamestown. One of the ships, as we afterward learned, was wrecked in a hurricane; seven arrived safely, and the ninth vessel we had not heard from.

All these people had expected to find food in plenty, servants to wait upon them, and everything furnished to hand without being obliged to raise a finger in their own behalf. What was yet worse, they had among them many men who believed they were to be made officers of the government.

THE NEW LAWS

NOW YOU MUST UNDERSTAND THAT WITH THE COMING of this fleet we of Jamestown were told that the London Company had changed all the laws for us in Virginia, and that Lord De la Warr, who sailed on the ship from which nothing had been heard, was to be our governor.

From that hour did it seem as if all the men in Jamestown, save only half a dozen, among whom were Captain Smith, Master Hunt and Master Percy, strove their best to wreck the settlement.

Because Lord De la Warr, the new governor, had not arrived, many of the new comers refused to obey my master, and they were so strong in numbers that it was not possible for him to force them to his will.

Each man strove for himself, regardless of the sick, or of the women and children. Some banded themselves together in companies, falling upon such Indian villages as they could easily overcome, and murdered and robbed until all the brown men of Virginia stood ready to shed the blood of every white man who crossed their path.

Then came that which plunged Nathaniel and me into deepest grief.

THE ACCIDENT

CAPTAIN SMITH HAD GONE UP THE BAY IN THE HOPE of soothing the trouble among the savages, and, failing in this effort, was returning, having got within four and twenty hours' journey of Jamestown, when the pinnace was anchored for the night.

The boat's company lay down to sleep, and then came that accident, if accident it may be called, the cause of which no man has ever been able to explain to the satisfaction of Master Hunt or myself.

Captain Smith was asleep, with his powder bag by his side, when in some manner it was set on fire, and the powder, exploding, tore

the flesh from his body and thighs for the space of nine or ten inches square, even down to the bones.

In his agony, and being thus horribly aroused from sleep, hardly knowing what he did, he plunged overboard as the quickest way to soothe the pain. There he was like to have drowned but for Samuel White, who came near to losing his own life in saving him.

He was brought back to the town on the day before the ships of the fleet, which had brought so many quarrelsome people, were to sail for England. With no surgeon to dress his wounds, what could he do but depart in one of these ships with the poor hope of living in agony until he arrived on the other side of the ocean.

Nathaniel and I would have gone with him, willing, because of his friendship for us, to have served him so long as we lived. He refused to listen to our prayers, insisting that we were lads well fitted to live in a new land like Virginia, and that if we would but remain with Master Hunt, working out our time of apprenticeship, which would be but five years longer, then might we find ourselves men of importance in the colony. He doubted not, so he said, but that we would continue, after he had gone, as we had while he was with us.

What could we lads do other than obey, when his commands were laid upon us, even though our hearts were so sore that it seemed as if it would no longer be possible to live when he had departed?

Even amid his suffering, when one might well have believed that he could give no heed to anything save his own plight, he spoke to us of what we should do for the bettering of our own condition. He promised that as soon as he was come to London, and able to walk around, if so be God permitted him to live, he would seek out Nathaniel's parents to tell them that the lad who had run away from his home was rapidly making a man of himself in Virginia, and would one day come back to gladden their hearts.

CAPTAIN SMITH'S DEPARTURE

It is not well for me to dwell upon our parting with the master whom we had served more than two years, and who had ever

been the most friendly friend and the most manly man one could ask to meet.

Our hearts were sore, when, after having done what little we might toward carrying him on board the ship, we came back to his house, which he had said in the presence of witnesses should be ours, and there took up our lives with Master Hunt.

But for that good man's prayers, on this first night we would have abandoned ourselves entirely to grief; but he devoted his time to soothing us, showing why we had no right to do other than continue in the course on which we had been started by the man who was gone from us, until it was, to my mind at least, as if I should be doing some grievous wrong to my master, if I failed to carry on the work while he was away, as it would have been done had I known we were to see him again within the week.

With Captain Smith gone, perhaps to his death; with half a dozen men who claimed the right to stand at the head of the government until Lord De la Warr should come; and with the savages menacing us on every hand, sore indeed was our plight.

With so many in the town, for there were now four hundred and ninety persons, and while the savages, because of having been so sorely wronged, were in arms against us, it was no longer possible to go abroad for food, and as the winter came on we were put to it even in that land of plenty, for enough to keep ourselves alive.

THE "STARVING TIME"

We came to know what starvation meant during that winter, and were I to set down here all of the suffering, of the hunger-weakness, and of the selfishness we saw during the six months after Captain Smith sailed for home, there would not be days enough left in my life to complete the tale.

As I look back on it now, it seems more like some wonderful dream than a reality, wherein men strove with women and children for food to keep life in their own worthless bodies.

It is enough if I say that of the four hundred and ninety persons whom Captain Smith left behind him, there were, in the month of May of the year 1610, but fifty-eight left alive. That God should have spared among those, Nathaniel Peacock and myself, is something which passeth understanding, for verily there were scores of better than we whose lives would have advantaged Jamestown more than

ours ever can, who died and were buried as best they could be by the few who had sufficient strength remaining to dig the graves.

I set it down in all truth that, through God's mercy, our lives were saved by Master Hunt, for he counseled us wisely as to the care we should take of our bodies when our stomachs were crying out for food, and it was he who showed us how we might prepare this herb or the bark from that tree for the sustaining of life, when we had nothing else to put into our mouths.

We had forgotten that Lord De la Warr was the new governor; we had heard nothing of the ship in which it was said Sir Thomas Gates and Sir George Somers had sailed. We were come to that pass where we cared neither for governor nor nobleman. We strove only to keep within our bodies the life which had become painful.

Then it was, when the few of us who yet lived, feared each moment lest the savages would put an end to us, that we saw sailing up into the bay two small ships, and I doubt if there was any among us who did not fall upon his knees and give thanks aloud to God for the help which had come at the very moment when it had seemed that we were past all aid.

OUR COURAGE GIVES OUT

But our time of rejoicing was short. Although these two ships were brought by Sir Thomas Gates and Sir George Somers, having in them not less than one hundred and fifty men, they did not have among them food sufficient to provide for the wants of our company until another harvest should come.

The vessel in which these new comers had sailed was, as I have said, wrecked in a hurricane near the Bermuda Isles, where, after much labor, they had contrived to build these two small ships.

It needed not that we, who of all our people in Jamestown remained alive, should tell the story of what we had suffered, for that could be read on our faces.

Neither was it required that these new comers should study long in order to decide upon the course to be pursued, for the answer to all their speculations could be found in the empty storehouse, and in the numberless graves 'twixt there and the river bank.

Of provisions, they had so much as might serve for a voyage to England, if peradventure the winds were favorable; and ere the ships had been at anchor four and twenty hours, it was resolved that we should abandon this town of James, which we had hoped might one day grow into a city fair to look upon.

An attempt to build up a nation in this new land of Virginia, of which ours was the third, had cost of money and of blood more than man could well set down, and now, after all this brave effort on the part of such men as Captain Smith, Master Hunt and Master Percy, it was to go for naught.

Once more were the savages to hold undisputed possession of the land which they claimed as their own.

ABANDONING JAMESTOWN

Now even though Nathaniel Peacock and I had known more of suffering and of sorrow, than of pleasure, in Jamestown, our hearts were sore at leaving it.

It seemed to me as if we were running contrary to that which my master would have commanded, and there were tears in my eyes, of which I was not ashamed, when Nathaniel and I, hand in hand, followed Master Hunt out of the house we had helped to build.

Those who had come from the shipwreck amid the Bermudas,

were rejoicing because they had failed to arrive in time to share with us the starvation and the sickness, therefore to them this turning back upon the enterprise was but a piece of good fortune. Yet were they silent and sad, understanding our sorrow.

It was the eighth day of June, in the year 1610, when we set sail from Jamestown, believing we were done with the new world forever, and yet within less than three hours was all our grief changed to rejoicing, all our sorrow to thankfulness.

LORD DE LA WARR'S ARRIVAL

At the mouth of the river, sailing toward us bravely as if having come from some glorious victory, were three ships laden with men, and, as we afterward came to know, an ample store of provisions.

It was Lord De la Warr who had come to take up his governorship, and verily he was arrived in the very point of time, for had he been delayed four and twenty hours, we would have been on the ocean, where was little likelihood of seeing him.

It needs not I should say that our ships were turned back, and before nightfall Master Hunt was sitting in Captain Smith's house, with Nathaniel Peacock and me cooking for him such a dinner as we

three had not known these six months past.

I have finished my story of Jamestown, having set myself to tell only of what was done there while we were with Captain John Smith.

And it is well I should bring this story to an end here, for if I make any attempt at telling what came to Nathaniel Peacock and myself after that, then am I like to keep on until he who has begun to read will lay down the story because of weariness.

For the satisfaction of myself, and the better pleasing of Nathaniel Peacock, however, I will add, concerning our two selves, that we remained in the land of Virginia until our time of apprenticeship was ended, and then it was, that Master Hunt did for us as Captain Smith had promised to do.

THE YOUNG PLANTERS

WE FOUND OURSELVES, IN THE YEAR 1614, the owners of an hundred acres of land which Nathaniel and I had chosen some distance back from the river, so that we might stand in no danger of the shaking sickness, and built ourselves a house like unto the one we had helped make for Captain Smith.

With the coming of Lord De la Warr all things were changed. The governing of the people was done as my old master, who never saw Virginia again, I grieve to say, would have had it. We became a law-abiding people, save when a few hotheads stirred up trouble and got the worst of it.

When Nathaniel Peacock and I settled down as planters on our own account, there were eleven villages in the land of Virginia, and, living in them, more than four thousand men, women, and children.

It was no longer a country over which the savages ruled without check, though sad to relate, the brown men of the land shed the blood of white men like water, ere they were driven out from among us.

It is well I set down here at the end, that but for Captain John Smith and Master Hunt, Nathaniel Peacock and I might have remained in London to become worthless vagabonds, whereas we stand today free men, planters who are fairly well respected among our fellows; and I hope, as well as believe, that no man within this land of Virginia can say that he was ever wronged or made sorrowful by Nathaniel Peacock or by Richard of Jamestown.

www.ingramcontent.com/pod-product-compliance
Ingram Content Group UK Ltd.
Pitfield, Milton Keynes, MK11 3LW, UK
UKHW041953230426
12048UKWH00008B/315